50 Days in an Adventure in the book of Romans

By

Paul Sutliff

©2020,

Paul Sutliff

All scriptures come from the King James Version. The modern use of "You" has been substituted replacing "you," "you," "your," "your." Old English endings have also been removed to make the reading easier.

Dedication

This book is dedicated to my beautiful children David, Jennifer and John. You are loved. May you forever find happiness.

Thank you to all of those at Hope Christian Fellowship in Rochester, NY who have given me endless hours of love, devotion and happiness sharing in my trials, needs, prayers and more. I can never repay you for your boundless love.

SPECIAL NOTE

This devotional has video links to YouTube videos for each day. Those who have difficulty reading may find this it easier to listen than to read.

About the Author

Paul Sutliff is a retired special education teacher who has been enjoying the fellowship at Hope Christian Fellowship in Rochester, NY. Paul is also a published research writer in the field on national security issues that involve Islamization and immigration. Paul does a weekly Christian News radio show on Thursdays at 6:00pm Eastern Time on BlogTalkRadio.com via Global Patriot Radio.

Paul loves apologetics so much he teaches Apologetics whenever he gets a chance. He has created a 10-week class of immersion into Apologetics that he calls the Evangelist's Toolbox.

This is Paul's third devotional. If you like this one, pick up his devotional on the book of Mark.

DAY #1
ROMANS 1:1-7
https://www.youtube.com/watch?v=xWLsp4ROodg

1 Paul, a bondservant of Jesus Christ, called [to be] an apostle, separated to the gospel of God

2 which He promised before through His prophets in the Holy Scriptures,

3 concerning His Son Jesus Christ our Lord, who was born of the seed of David according to the flesh,

4 [and] declared [to be] the Son of God with power according to the Spirit of holiness, by the resurrection from the dead.

5 Through Him we have received grace and apostleship for obedience to the faith among all nations for His name,

6 among whom you also are the called of Jesus Christ;

7 To all who are in Rome, beloved of God, called [to be] saints: Grace to you and peace from God our Father and the Lord Jesus Christ.

These seven verses are Paul's introduction to the Romans. In this short introduction he reveals himself to be a follower of Jesus and a scholar of the Old Testament or a rabbi. He shows that he has a personal relationship with Jesus and by what authority he writes having spoken of being an apostle for Lord Jesus.

Paul does not waste words, there is not one word here wasted. Not one flowery word that could be forgotten or dismissed. There is so much here that testifies he is indeed a follower of Jesus. He shows that he is saved by grace. There was nothing he did to deserve Jesus. Yet it was the power of God Almighty that saved him and made him an apostle for Christ. Every word in these seven verses shares that he knows who the savior is. Every word cries out he has found a love of the Messiah and the greatness of the living God that cannot be measured by our mortal minds.

Paul even uses the correct greeting to those who serve and follow Jesus! He calls them saints! Saints are those living in Christ! Sadly, some churches have stolen this term that belongs to the living and have assigned it to the dead. It makes no sense to write a letter to the dead. Paul was clearly writing to the living. His greeting "Grace to you and peace from God our Father and the Lord Jesus Christ," speak of his personal joy in being a Christian. Paul is living in the grace and peace of God! Is that not what all Christians are doing? Are you not living in a state of forgiveness thanks to the finished work of Jesus? Has God not granted you peace? If you answered no to this, be encouraged that Jesus stands knocking at the door of your heart, waiting on you to say, "yes Lord, I accept that you died for my sins. You gave your life so my sins could be forgiven. Lord, thank you for doing this for me. Thank you for giving your all for me. Thank you, Jesus. Now be Lord of my life."

Dear Lord Jesus,

You gave your life for me long before my parents and their parents were even born. You thought of me even then. Help me Lord Jesus to live a life pleasing to You. Help me Lord in my foolishness to make the right choices. Help me to seek Your wisdom and not my own. Help me to say no to evil and choose to let Your let shine in that darkness that is this world. God please guide my footsteps.

In Jesus name, Amen.

DAY #2
ROMANS 1:8-17
https://www.youtube.com/watch?v=fO37CwHDV6g

8	First, I thank my God through Jesus Christ for you all, that your faith is spoken of throughout the whole world.
9	For God is my witness, whom I serve with my spirit in the gospel of His Son, that without ceasing I make mention of you always in my prayers,
10	making request if, by some means, now at last I may find a way in the will of God to come to you.
11	For I long to see you, that I may impart to you some spiritual gift, so that you may be established—
12	that is, that I may be encouraged together with you by the mutual faith both of you and me.
13	Now I do not want you to be unaware, brethren, that I often planned to come to you (but was hindered until now), that I might have some fruit among you also, just as among the other Gentiles.
14	I am a debtor both to Greeks and to barbarians, both to wise and to unwise.
15	So, as much as is in me, [I am] ready to preach the gospel to you who are in Rome also.
16	For I am not ashamed of the gospel of Christ, for it is the power of God to salvation for everyone who believes, for the Jew first and also for the Greek.
17	For in it the righteousness of God is revealed from faith to faith; as it is written, "The just shall live by faith."

Paul, having introduced himself, begins by telling those he is writing to that they are in his daily prayers. He gives thanks to God for their faith that has reached far beyond the city of Rome. Paul is talking about the joy the good news delivers that is exciting. It excites your very soul when one person comes to Christ. To think that in what was the den of idolatry, the very seat of paganism, that Almighty God, had already sent His GOOD NEWS of Jesus. Paul knew that their love of Jesus also had risks. The faith of those in Rome in Jesus was a very dangerous thing. Still, his daily prayers asked our loving God to send him into what was seen to Jews as a den of iniquity, a place of paganism, one of the cores of evil upon the planet. Paul says his selfishness is to give the believers something special from God first. Then he shares his hope of an opportunity to share his love of the Messiah, Jesus our Lord with those in Rome who had yet to hear of the love of Christ, that even in that place of evil, some would come to know him. Paul knew of the risks this would bring. It meant he would be daily risking his life to share the Gospel and if found more than likely would mean his death. Still Paul sought God, to be this evangelist of His Word.

But Paul was not ashamed of the Gospel! He was unafraid to share His Word as many Christians today fear the loss of friends and family for sharing the Gospel. Paul only knew of its power to bring salvation to the lost. That joyful message of hope was all that mattered to him! Paul knew that if he did what he believed was his job in sharing the Gospel, that the Holy Spirit would not return void (Is. 55:11). That sharing the message of Hope found in the death and resurrection of Christ, the very righteousness of it would open the fog over the hearts of many to finally find reason to live as never before, creating the "Just" who would live by faith!

Dear Lord Jesus,

Thank you for those I know who have come to know You and who play such an important work in my life. Lord, I pray for my Pastor and those who keep me in their prayers. Lord, you know my heart. You know I want to share you and need your strength to do this boldly as Paul did. Lord awaken in me a desire to share your Good News, a desire to see the joy that is found in seeing one risk it all to find the glory in embracing Your love for us. Use me Lord, use me so others may find You!

In Jesus Name, Amen!

DAY #3
ROMANS 1:18-21
https://www.youtube.com/watch?v=NZw3Weka1rk

18   For the wrath of God is revealed from heaven against all ungodliness and unrighteousness of men, who suppress the truth in unrighteousness,

19   because what may be known of God is manifest in them, for God has shown [it] to them.

20   For since the creation of the world His invisible [attributes] are clearly seen, being understood by the things that are made, [even] His eternal power and Godhead, so that they are without excuse,

21   because, although they knew God, they did not glorify [Him] as God, nor were thankful, but became futile in their thoughts, and their foolish hearts were darkened.

Paul tells us that God's anger, His very wrath is directed against sin not people. God hates sin. Sin is the cause of the unrighteousness of men. The fact is, that there are people out there who do everything that they can, to stop people from learning from about truth. What truth? Truth—about who Jesus was and what he did for us.

In today's world there are many people who hide what is true from us. People on TV lie and tell us things that they know are not true. Politicians lie to us to get us to believe in them creating votes. But the worst of all is those who do what they can to keep people from learning who Jesus is. In America, the very action of preventing others from knowing who Jesus was, was considered a violation of our Freedom of Religion until recently. It was considered by many to be one of the most horrible crimes that should not be committed. But with the advent of video on the internet this has become worse. Add in the period of American history, which likely will be called "the time of Insanity," when the Wuhan Virus spread, and the specific orders of governors across the USA were directed against churches to keep people from gathering and learning about Jesus.

Verse 19 is in many ways a sorrowful reveal of truth about those who would keep us from a saving knowledge of Jesus Christ. It tells us that these people KNOW that truth and do everything to keep others from learning it!

Verse 20 talks about the invisible attributes of God. One of the amazing truths about the universe is a bunch of rules, that are the rules of the science of knowledge, called Logic. God is the master, the very creator of these rules that are called Logic. Logic tells us when someone is lying. It tells us when people are practicing to deceive us. Logic also shows us how others are "illogical" in their communication. For many of us older persons who grew up watching shows like Star Trek, the very talk of logic brings to mind a pointed eared character called Spock who strived to live and breathe only logic. He was cold in his demeanor, but there was no one you trusted more to tell the truth. Logic helps us to know who God is, and what he has done for us. The Master of Logic, the Great Creator shows us with these rules that men who wish to hide who Jesus is amy have a personal reason for not accepting the reality of who Jesus is, but in truth have no reason for hiding what is true from us.

Politicians may lie to us to get us not to elect opponent. But hiding truth from us is an expression that we are too stupid to find out what the truth is. Hiding who God is, when so much of nature declares who he is to us is nothing but foolish. As simple as it is, God is truth. He is light. Darkness is the absence of light. Darkness disappears wherever light appears. Darkness never takes over light!

Dear Lord Jesus!

I praise you that you alone are worthy of my praise. Thank you for Your Word that shines as a light in the darkness. Thank you for giving us Your Word that I may know more about You. Thank you for sending Your son Jesus that I may be forgiven of my sins! Lord please use me. Lord I ask that you take my vanity, take my foolishness, and guide me that I, like Paul, may draw others to you.

In Jesus Name, Amen.

DAY #4
ROMANS 1:22-32
https://www.youtube.com/watch?v=Gqj947DJfRE

22 Professing to be wise, they became fools,

23 and changed the glory of the incorruptible God into an image made like corruptible man--and birds and four-footed animals and creeping things.

24 Therefore God also gave them up to uncleanness, in the lusts of their hearts, to dishonor their bodies among themselves,

25 who exchanged the truth of God for the lie, and worshiped and served the creature rather than the Creator, who is blessed forever. Amen.

26 For this reason God gave them up to vile passions. For even their women exchanged the natural use for what is against nature.

27 Likewise also the men, leaving the natural use of the woman, burned in their lust for one another, men with men committing what is shameful, and receiving in themselves the penalty of their error which was due.

28 And even as they did not like to retain God in [their] knowledge, God gave them over to a debased mind, to do those things which are not fitting;

29 being filled with all unrighteousness, sexual immorality, wickedness, covetousness, maliciousness; full of envy, murder, strife, deceit, evil-mindedness; [they are] whisperers,

30 backbiters, haters of God, violent, proud, boasters, inventors of evil things, disobedient to parents,

31 undiscerning, untrustworthy, unloving, unforgiving, unmerciful;

32 who, knowing the righteous judgment of God, that those who practice such things are deserving of death, not only do the same but also approve of those who practice them.

Those who knew God and do not praise, glorify or anyway give him the honor he is due, exchange their wisdom for foolishness. They may teach, have positions of authority, be considered "wise" but the moment they choose knowingly to not honor Jesus as God after they know who he was, they chose foolishness over wisdom.

Many of those who chose this way choose to portray God in a manner which is easy for them. Some make pictures to mock God, some make idols. The desire of their hearts stands opposed to the God who loves them. God could simply choose to force them to acknowledge Him. But, being the God of love, He allows them to make the choices to follow Him or to follow darkness.

Choices have consequences. Sadly, this is more true than most of us want to admit. Choosing wrong here means God leaves you to your choice and that leads down the rabbit hole into sexual confusion of what is good versus bad. Homosexuality was a normal pleasure in Rome and Greece. It was not viewed as abnormal.

But the list goes far beyond perversity. The list encompasses many things that push a person away from society, forcing them to only socialize with others of like corrupt minds, that do not seek to help others but to harm them.

Dear Lord Jesus,

Guide my footsteps so that I may magnify Your name and NOT choose foolishness. Lord guide me in to the loving embrace of Your open arms. Help me to see that your ways are the best. Use me Lord, that I may help direct others to that need to know your loving embrace.

In Jesus name, Amen.

DAY #5
ROMANS 2:1-11
https://www.youtube.com/watch?v=YTAgyLLFtxg

1. Therefore you are inexcusable, O man, whoever you are who judge, for in whatever you judge another you condemn yourself; for you who judge practice the same things.
2. But we know that the judgment of God is according to truth against those who practice such things.
3. And do you think this, O man, you who judge those practicing such things, and doing the same, that you will escape the judgment of God?

4   Or do you despise the riches of His goodness, forbearance, and longsuffering, not knowing that the goodness of God leads you to repentance?
5   But in accordance with your hardness and your impenitent heart you are treasuring up for yourself wrath in the day of wrath and revelation of the righteous judgment of God,
6   who "will render to each one according to his deeds":
7   eternal life to those who by patient continuance in doing good seek for glory, honor, and immortality;
8   but to those who are self-seeking and do not obey the truth, but obey unrighteousness--indignation and wrath,
9   tribulation and anguish, on every soul of man who does evil, of the Jew first and also of the Greek;
10 but glory, honor, and peace to everyone who works what is good, to the Jew first and also to the Greek.
11 For there is no partiality with God.

Today when you read the news it is no longer surprising to hear of judges committing crimes for which they passed judgement on others. This should be seen as the horror it is, that someone who is supposed to be wise and an example of the law was only a pretender. But their judgement is nothing compared to the one and only God whose judgement is perfect and true. There is no escaping His decisions. Where can one flee from God's courtroom? Better still is that in God's perfect judgement there is goodness. His love, His righteousness being that which leads all of us sinners to find Christ. So, God rewards those who follow Him with eternal life! But this loving God even gives more than this promise to those who love Him, Jesus tells us of mansions prepared for us!

Sadly, there are those who choose not to accept the work of Christ upon the cross as the sacrifice for their sins. The persist in seeking evil. Their selfishness is caught up on seeking pleasures only for them. They care not for those around them. Their reward is also promised. A reward of eternal punishment.

Paul says of the judgements to the "Jew first and then to the "Greek." He places blame and reward upon Jews first because they had the Torah (Law), the Kethubim (Writings) and the Navim (Prophets) which is what Christians call the Old Testament. God chose them so they have no excuse to ignore His Word. But even in this Paul tells us there is no partiality in God. God is fair and impartial. Its all up to you to choose to follow him or not.

Dear Lord Jesus!

Help me to seek to do your will. Help me to put others first, help me to see the needs of others before my own. Lord, guide me into becoming a great lover of your pleasure rather than my own! Mold me and make me into one who stands on Your word as an example to those new in Christ and as a beacon of Your loving kindness. Lord, let me the one who plants seeds so others may find Your great love.

In Jesus name, Amen.

DAY #6
ROMANS 2:12-24
https://www.youtube.com/watch?v=kM-2j5TVoFA

12   For as many as have sinned without law will also perish without law, and as many as have sinned in the law will be judged by the law

13   (for not the hearers of the law [are] just in the sight of God, but the doers of the law will be justified;

50 DAYS IN ROMANS

14 for when Gentiles, who do not have the law, by nature do the things in the law, these, although not having the law, are a law to themselves,

15 who show the work of the law written in their hearts, their conscience also bearing witness, and between themselves [their] thoughts accusing or else excusing [them])

16 in the day when God will judge the secrets of men by Jesus Christ, according to my gospel.

17 Indeed you are called a Jew, and rest on the law, and make your boast in God,

18 and know [His] will, and approve the things that are excellent, being instructed out of the law,

19 and are confident that you yourself are a guide to the blind, a light to those who are in darkness,

20 an instructor of the foolish, a teacher of babes, having the form of knowledge and truth in the law.

21 You, therefore, who teach another, do you not teach yourself? You who preach that a man should not steal, do you steal?

22 You who say, "Do not commit adultery," do you commit adultery? You who abhor idols, do you rob temples?

23 You who make your boast in the law, do you dishonor God through breaking the law?

24 For "the name of God is blasphemed among the Gentiles because of you," as it is written.

Basically, this means both Jews and Gentiles are guilty of violating the law of God and are sinners. Actual goodness is

impossible, because when we break God's law we deserve the penalty. Even those who hear God's word are guilty. During this time period, the Jews felt themselves special almost of a haughty type nature because God chose them. Some took this to mean they could do whatever they want. They really could not avoid hearing God's Word. They heard it but they do not allow it to take fruit and grow. Paul here condemns the Jew alongside the Gentile who is ignorant of the law. He also praises those who by nature were following God's laws, who had no idea that was what they were doing.

The big message here is that hearing the Word is important but if the person hearing the word does nothing with it, it is no better than a seed that does not bear fruit. What then, how can a person do more with what they hear or read? In order for the Word of God to do more, you must first take that step of faith and believe Jesus was who He claimed to be. The Messiah, the great and Almighty God, who gave his (human) life that We may life eternal. Next, be serious about setting aside time to be with God. Take time to read and study. Think on the words found in the scriptures, and yes, pray over them as you think.

Dear Lord Jesus,

You love us so much you sent us guidance in the form of your Bible. Your Word, changed my heart. You bought me with your blood. Then You went beyond that and gave me a guidebook on how to live life fully. Lord, help me to understand Your Word. Help me to continually keep Your Word in my heart. Lord, may Your Word be fresh within me as a well springing up so that I may share your love with others.

In Jesus name, Amen.

DAY #7
ROMANS 2:25-3:9
https://www.youtube.com/watch?v=hh6CGGiIBaw

25 For circumcision is indeed profitable if you keep the law; but if you are a breaker of the law, your circumcision has become uncircumcision.

26 Therefore, if an uncircumcised man keeps the righteous requirements of the law, will not his uncircumcision be counted as circumcision?

27 And will not the physically uncircumcised, if he fulfills the law, judge you who, [even] with [your] written [code] and circumcision, [are] a transgressor of the law?

28 For he is not a Jew who [is one] outwardly, nor [is] circumcision that which [is] outward in the flesh;

29 but [he is] a Jew who [is one] inwardly; and circumcision [is that] of the heart, in the Spirit, not in the letter; whose praise [is] not from men but from God.

3:1 What advantage then has the Jew, or what [is] the profit of circumcision?

2 Much in every way! Chiefly because to them were committed the oracles of God.

3 For what if some did not believe? Will their unbelief make the faithfulness of God without effect?

4 Certainly not! Indeed, let God be true but every man a liar. As it is written: "That You may be justified in Your words, And may overcome when You are judged."

5 But if our unrighteousness demonstrates the righteousness of God, what shall we say? [Is] God unjust who inflicts wrath? (I speak as a man.)

6	Certainly not! For then how will God judge the world?
7	For if the truth of God has increased through my lie to His glory, why am I also still judged as a sinner?
8	And [why] not [say], "Let us do evil that good may come"?--as we are slanderously reported and as some affirm that we say. Their condemnation is just.
9	What then? Are we better [than they]? Not at all. For we have previously charged both Jews and Greeks that they are all under sin.

To the Jews, there was reason to celebrate what set them apart from others. For the males circumcision strongly designated who they were. It was not something their enemies did not know about also. They celebrated circumcision and they still do today as an act that separates them as God's chosen people. An act of outward expression of being Jewish. An act of submission to doing as God requested to designate who they are.

But many Jews saw this as an action that went beyond and was in many ways their salvation. Being set apart physically however was not a circumcision of the heart. The Jews needed Jesus just as the Gentiles. Many Jews knew the needed a Messiah, but did not understand that this Messiah came to change their hearts. They thought the Messiah was coming to save them physically through putting down their oppressors, the Romans.

This passage-could only be written by a Jew to those who are Jewish. Paul knew of how the Jews thought. He knew of the self-important belief, the self-salvation belief that came from a belief their circumcision was their salvation. But without a changed heart by the work of the Messiah it was all for nothing.

Dear Lord Jesus,

Praise God, your perfectness reveals my imperfection, my unworthiness of your great love. Lord there is nothing, nothing that makes me worthy. Not circumcision, not acts of kindness and mercy, nothing that makes me worthy of your loving kindness. Thank you for what you did on the cross for me. Praise YOU for all you have done for us knowing how unworthy we are of Your love. Lord, Your love, Your kindness, Your sacrifice are all more than I deserve. Never let me forget that Love. Help me Lord to share how Your love has changed my own life.

In Jesus name, Amen.

DAY #8
ROMANS 3:10-20

https://www.youtube.com/watch?v=60_wlnkMfZg

10   As it is written: "There is none righteous, no, not one;

11   There is none who understands; There is none who seeks after God.

12   They have all turned aside; They have together become unprofitable; There is none who does good, no, not one."

13   "Their throat [is] an open tomb; With their tongues they have practiced deceit"; "The poison of asps [is] under their lips";

14   "Whose mouth [is] full of cursing and bitterness."

15   "Their feet [are] swift to shed blood;

16   Destruction and misery [are] in their ways;

17   And the way of peace they have not known."

18   "There is no fear of God before their eyes."

19 Now we know that whatever the law says, it says to those who are under the law, that every mouth may be stopped, and all the world may become guilty before God.

20 Therefore by the deeds of the law no flesh will be justified in His sight, for by the law [is] the knowledge of sin.

Who can claim to do good and to be saved by their good deeds if not one is righteous? Who can say I am justified by the amount of good deeds, or by the amount of money I give to charity, or by the amount of time I volunteer to help the needy? Not one! Every one of us is lacking in righteousness and laden with the guilt our sinfulness causes us to carry. In all of us, we have chosen our own selfish desires over God. We have chosen to lie instead of speak what is true. We have allowed our minds, if only that, to fantasize about responding to others in a bloody rage rather than choosing a response that is filled with God's grace. So many of our thoughts, if only that, betray us as living without a fear of God. The Law, tells us of our sins. It points directly at the sins we have committed, NAMING THEM! God laid out simple directions in the giving of His law, and still we remained seekers of sin. There is nothing—nothing we can do to deserve the grace of God. No flesh is justified in the sight of God by the law. It points out our sinfulness.

It is Jesus alone. Jesus, God in the flesh, who came to us, showed us how to live, then offered His life as a living sacrifice, for no other reason than His great love for us.

Dear Lord Jesus,

There are many that say they are saved by the amount of good deeds they do vs. the amount of bad things they do. Lord, this passage written almost 2,000 years ago was written so that they can know their goodness is filth. When we are stained with guilt of sin, we cannot be justified by our deeds. Your love, God, is so great. You alone are worthy of praise, for You Lord Jesus saw us in our sin and still offered Your life for us to be forgiven of that horrible crime. Lord, use me. Use me that I may be an example so that others may see you. Use me that I may share your love to others.

In Jesus name, Amen.

DAY #9
ROMANS 3:21-31
https://www.youtube.com/watch?v=TTtnA7AUDuU

21   But now the righteousness of God without the law is manifested, being witnessed by the law and the prophets;

22   Even the righteousness of God [which is] by faith of Jesus Christ unto all and upon all them that believe: for there is no difference:

23   For all have sinned, and come short of the glory of God;

24   Being justified freely by his grace through the redemption that is in Christ Jesus:

25   Whom God hath set forth [to be] a propitiation through faith in his blood, to declare his righteousness for the remission of sins that are past, through the forbearance of God;

26   To declare, [I say], at this time his righteousness: that he might be just, and the justifier of him which believeth in Jesus.

27   Where [is] boasting then? It is excluded. By what law? of works? Nay: but by the law of faith.

28   Therefore we conclude that a man is justified by faith without the deeds of the law.

29   [Is he] the God of the Jews only? [is he] not also of the Gentiles? Yes, of the Gentiles also:

30   Seeing [it is] one God, which shall justify the circumcision by faith, and uncircumcision through faith.

31   Do we then make void the law through faith? God forbid: yea, we establish the law.

Only God is righteous. Before the law existed, God's actions were witnessed. When the law was written it proclaims His knowledge and His righteousness while at the same time revealing the very sorry state of man. Man, the creation of God, who has trouble doing what is righteous. Man carries that stain, that horrible stench of disobedience to the one who is righteous. Man carries that undeniable desire to what the law proclaims as ungodly and sinful. None of us can deny having engaged in some form of sin. We all bear the weight of our own sin.----

Unless----You have given your life to the one who is holy and righteous. To that one who shed His own blood that you may have life eternal. The great God, the I AM, come in the flesh in the person of Jesus Christ, came to live his life as an example and to give us the one thing we could not attain by ourselves. Life eternal.

Mankind has done nothing to deserve their freedom from the stain of sin. WE have done nothing to deserve this kind of love. Yet Christ our Lord showed his love to us by dying and taking on the role of the perfect sacrifice for our sins that we may no longer be prevented from partaking in the joys that lay in the hereafter in His presence.

Yet there are men who would say you must do this or that to receive salvation. They make it dependent on how you dress, what you do, how much you give, and if you do miss time at their gatherings. Those who live under this boast in their own goodness. We who know the Bible, can make boast in the things we do as if they would save us. We may be proud of things we do and rightly so. But not one of those things could save us from the deserved punishment for our sins.

If we must boast we must boast of what Jesus has done for us! Is that not what He desires of us? That we would share His passion and His love for sinners as he loved us while we were yet in our sins.

Dear Lord Jesus,

May You alone be praised for such selfless love that dared to love even a sinner like me. You gave your life for me. You shed your blood that I might be freed from the wages I earned from my sins. Lord, use even me that I may share of Your wonder and glory. That I may somehow in some way lead others to know a God who loves them before they even know that God is pursuing them that they may know His glory and wonder.

In Jesus Name, Amen.

DAY 10
ROMANS 4:1-8
https://www.youtube.com/watch?v=9Jj6QV-j0W0

1. What then shall we say that Abraham our father has found according to the flesh?

2. For if Abraham was justified by works, he has [something] to boast about, but not before God.

3. For what does the Scripture say? "Abraham believed God, and it was accounted to him for righteousness."

4. Now to him who works, the wages are not counted as grace but as debt.

5	But to him who does not work but believes on Him who justifies the ungodly, his faith is accounted for righteousness,
6	just as David also describes the blessedness of the man to whom God imputes righteousness apart from works:
7	"Blessed [are those] whose lawless deeds are forgiven, And whose sins are covered;
8	Blessed [is the] man to whom the LORD shall not impute sin."

The differences between a God worthy of our worship and a god made by human hands are so vast and numerous that they are truly incomparable. What kind of a god owes man? If our righteousness comes not from God but from our good deeds does not God owe man? Would this type of god have rules that rule over him? Would not a man justified by works be able to overturn the penalties of sin for crimes like rape and murder by simply doing good deeds? How empty would Hell be if people simply had to do x amount of good deeds to get out of eternal punishment they deserve?

The flip side is the God of the Bible. This God warns you that you deserve Hell. You deserve eternal punishment for your sins. There is nothing that you can do, that makes you cleansed from your sins. NOTHING! No good work imaginable can save you from a second death where you live eternally because of your sinful nature. BUT this God of the Bible loves mankind. He, Himself sees man in his sin and seeks man's justification and redemption from this horrible penalty for sin. We are unworthy of this type of love because we in our sinful nature did not listen to God's warnings. We did not listen to His cries to not sin, and still very often do what is sinful when we know better. This loving God, comes to earth, and dies in our place paying the penalty for our sins. He alone was worthy to pay that penalty. Now what is the cost of such redemption for a man or woman? What price must they pay to receive this "get out of Hell free card?" We are not fools, we know everything has a price. How many good deeds? How many prayers---? Wait---That brings us back to a god unworthy of our worship! So, what is the price? You must believe in Jesus and his sacrifice for your sins. Belief? Belief is all? That means if anything the work of God leaves us in debt to God for His great love. Yes, we truly have a God worthy of worship.

Dear Lord Jesus,

You alone are worthy of our love. You alone have paid the price for my sin. You alone are worthy of my worship. Lord, please use me. Show me how and what I must do to direct those who do not know you to the wonderous love you have for us. Most merciful savior, use me that others may discover how great your love is.

In Jesus name, Amen.

DAY 11
ROMANS 4:9-25
https://www.youtube.com/watch?v=M9eoZFvXcR4

9   [Does] this blessedness then [come] upon the circumcised [only], or upon the uncircumcised also? For we say that faith was accounted to Abraham for righteousness.

10   How then was it accounted? While he was circumcised, or uncircumcised? Not while circumcised, but while uncircumcised.

11   And he received the sign of circumcision, a seal of the righteousness of the faith which [he had while still] uncircumcised, that he might be the father of all those who

	believe, though they are uncircumcised, that righteousness might be imputed to them also,
12	and the father of circumcision to those who not only [are] of the circumcision, but who also walk in the steps of the faith which our father Abraham [had while still] uncircumcised.
13	For the promise that he would be the heir of the world [was] not to Abraham or to his seed through the law, but through the righteousness of faith.
14	For if those who are of the law [are] heirs, faith is made void and the promise made of no effect,
15	because the law brings about wrath; for where there is no law [there is] no transgression.
16	Therefore [it is] of faith that [it might be] according to grace, so that the promise might be sure to all the seed, not only to those who are of the law, but also to those who are of the faith of Abraham, who is the father of us all
17	(as it is written, "I have made you a father of many nations") in the presence of Him whom he believed--God, who gives life to the dead and calls those things which do not exist as though they did;
18	who, contrary to hope, in hope believed, so that he became the father of many nations, according to what was spoken, "So shall your descendants be."
19	And not being weak in faith, he did not consider his own body, already dead (since he was about a hundred years old), and the deadness of Sarah's womb.
20	He did not waver at the promise of God through unbelief, but was strengthened in faith, giving glory to God,

21   and being fully convinced that what He had promised He was also able to perform.

22   And therefore "it was accounted to him for righteousness."

23   Now it was not written for his sake alone that it was imputed to him,

24   but also for us. It shall be imputed to us who believe in Him who raised up Jesus our Lord from the dead,

25   who was delivered up because of our offenses, and was raised because of our justification.

If you are not Jewish and are reading this, imagine that you were marked discreetly (in a hidden place on your person) as a child shortly after birth. You have been told that this mark is a symbol of your being chosen by God. Over time the word symbol falls from the communication about being chosen. You begin to place thankfulness to the circumcision and believe that the mark gives righteousness and not God. The Jewish men felt this mark set them above others. Yet they knew it was a mark, a work of man. Even the heritage of the Jewish people stretching back to Abraham was based not on works, but of faith. The Roman Jews needed a firm reminder of this. It almost seems that they thought themselves above other Christians. But it is faith and faith alone on our part that allows us as Believers to find salvation.

Abraham's importance to Judaism is not in being the first circumcised, but in being one of the first men to live his faith. He believed what God told him. He acted on his faith in God's words! Is this any less what men and do when they accept Christ's work on the cross as their sacrifice for their sins? This simple act of acceptance, an act of faith, is all that is required for salvation.

Dear Lord Jesus!

You alone are the author and finisher of our faith. You alone provided solace to us while we wallowed in the mire of unbelief and sin. It is only through Your love of me, that I am made whole. Use me God, to share your message of love to those who do not yet know you. Help me Lord to tell of what You have done in my life.

In Jesus name, Amen.

DAY #12
ROMANS 5:1-8

https://www.youtube.com/watch?v=hmb5M1Z2rn0

1   Therefore being justified by faith, we have peace with God through our Lord Jesus Christ:
2   By whom also we have access by faith into this grace wherein we stand, and rejoice in hope of the glory of God.
3   And not only [so], but we glory in tribulations also: knowing that tribulation works patience;
4   And patience, experience; and experience, hope:
5   And hope makes not ashamed; because the love of God is shed abroad in our hearts by the Holy Ghost which is given unto us.
6   For when we were yet without strength, in due time Christ died for the ungodly.
7   For scarcely for a righteous man will one die: yet peradventure for a good man some would even dare to die.
8   **But God commends his love toward us, in that, while we were yet sinners, Christ died for us.**

This incredible God we serve loves us so much that His love for us is sacrificial and goes beyond our limited understanding. His actions of love allow us to be justified by our faith in HIM. There is nothing we can do but believe. Something so simple, but yet so hard for so many. This simple expression of faith leads many of us to become willing to be persecuted for HIS sake. Why would an expression of our faith in HIS love lead us to endure hardship?

It is because we have done it all and we deserve nothing of the forgiving grace he gives to us. The incredible, overwhelming nature of a God who loves each one of so much His work is personal to us. He did this just for YOU and me! Verse 8 tells of our horrible sins and more. Most of us never have our sins on display. But to God they are known. They would block our way to salvation. Yet, Christ died for us while we were still in our sins.

Dear Lord Jesus!

You came and died for me while I was yet in my sins. You did this for me! You knowing how unworthy I am of your love died so that I may have the gift of eternal life. Lord, guide me that I may share your great unwavering love with others. Use me that my smallness my glorify you and your boundless love.

In Jesus name, Amen.

DAY #13
ROMANS 5:9-11
https://www.youtube.com/watch?v=HgZjWhyMjsg

9   Much more then, being now justified by his blood, we shall be saved from wrath through him.

10   For if, when we were enemies, we were reconciled to God by the death of his Son, much more, being reconciled, we shall be saved by his life.

11   And not only [so], but we also joy in God through our Lord Jesus Christ, by whom we have now received the atonement.

Have you ever considered yourself an enemy of God? How about as a man or woman who willing did something you thought God would not like? What about being someone who acted and did not care what the results were? You simply made a choice and what ever happened, happened.

God created us with purpose. He gave us free will. So we can choose to listen to Him or ignore him. We can choose! Yet til that precious day where we make that choice to follow Him, we are counted as an enemy. Why simply because we are choosing that which is sinful by not recognizing the work of Christ in ourselves. Oh we may have chosen to acknowledge it with our brains. We may have simply said OK Jesus did die on the cross. But it meant nothing to us personally. We did not grasp how important that was to ourself!

Yet in spite of our wretchedness, despite our willful nature to NOT acknowledge what Jesus did for us, He still loved us and willingly walked that path to the cross. He could have called down armies of angels. But he thought of us and said "<Your name here> needs to be with me rejoicing in heaven. I do this so he/she can get a free pass to heaven and be with me eternally."

We may have thought ourselves at odds with God. We may have hated him. We may simply have not known who He is. But there was never a moment 2,000 some years ago where he did not think of us as he was nailed to the cross and shed his blood for our sins. That is love beyond description.

Dear Lord Jesus!

Please, please know that I am yours God. I am your servant. I am willing to follow your directions. Lead me. Show me what you want me to do. Can I do any less for you who offered your life that I too may be saved? You give me reason to smile as the sun rises. You paint the skies that proclaim your glory. Lord use me. Use me to share your love with others. Make me bolder!

In Jesus name, Amen.

DAY #14
ROMANS 5:12-21
https://www.youtube.com/watch?v=wiN34tPaVfw

12 Wherefore, as by one man sin entered into the world, and death by sin; and so death passed upon all men, for that all have sinned:

13 (For until the law sin was in the world: but sin is not imputed when there is no law.

14 Nevertheless death reigned from Adam to Moses, even over them that had not sinned after the similitude of Adam's transgression, who is the figure of him that was to come.

15 But not as the offence, so also [is] the free gift. For if through the offence of one many be dead, much more the grace of God, and the gift by grace, [which is] by one man, Jesus Christ, hath abounded unto many.

16 And not as [it was] by one that sinned, [so is] the gift: for the judgment [was] by one to condemnation, but the free gift [is] of many offences unto justification.

17	For if by one man's offence death reigned by one; much more they which receive abundance of grace and of the gift of righteousness shall reign in life by one, Jesus Christ.)
18	Therefore as by the offence of one [judgment came] upon all men to condemnation; even so by the righteousness of one [the free gift came] upon all men unto justification of life.
19	For as by one man's disobedience many were made sinners, so by the obedience of one shall many be made righteous.
20	Moreover the law entered, that the offence might abound. But where sin abounded, grace did much more abound:
21	That as sin hath reigned unto death, even so might grace reign through righteousness unto eternal life by Jesus Christ our Lord.

God's plan for salvation is explained here. Through Adam sin entered the world. All of humanity became infected. But man was not charged with the crime of sin, because until Moses came and wrote the law, there was technically no crime to charge. This makes so much sense. You can't write a law and charge people with the crime of breaking that law before the law was written. Even though it was written in their hearts, the law was yet to be written.

One man, Adam brought sin into the world. One man brought salvation to the world, Jesus. Paul here talks about salvation as "the gift." When you give gifts you expect nothing in return. People give gifts on holidays and birthdays today. Salvation was freely given to us, Jesus does not say to us, ok you can have salvation if you do this, that, and the other thing. Something is not a gift if you have to work for it. That would make it a reward for labor, essentially a payment. Salvation is a gift! How much greater is this gift!

Dear Lord Jesus!

You alone deserve my praise. You alone offer me the gift of salvation. Lord, use me to share this simple message today. Help me to tell others of your gift given to all the world. Use me to share your gift of salvation. Use me that others may find your love.

In Jesus name, Amen.

DAY #15
ROMANS 6:1-11
https://www.youtube.com/watch?v=MiwclqtlLnk

1   What shall we say then? Shall we continue in sin, that grace may abound?

2   God forbid. How shall we, that are dead to sin, live any longer therein?

3   Know you not, that so many of us as were baptized into Jesus Christ were baptized into his death?

4   Therefore we are buried with him by baptism into death: that like as Christ was raised up from the dead by the glory of the Father, even so we also should walk in newness of life.

5   For if we have been planted together in the likeness of his death, we shall be also [in the likeness] of [his] resurrection:

6	Knowing this, that our old man is crucified with [him], that the body of sin might be destroyed, that henceforth we should not serve sin.
7	For he that is dead is freed from sin.
8	Now if we be dead with Christ, we believe that we shall also live with him:
9	Knowing that Christ being raised from the dead dies no more; death hath no more dominion over him.
10	For in that he died, he died unto sin once: but in that he lives, he lives unto God.
11	Likewise reckon you also yourselves to be dead indeed unto sin, but alive unto God through Jesus Christ our Lord.

The truth is that sinning after choosing Christ we tend to know we are sinning. Christians know they should do better. Christians know they should not sin. Worse, we know that once you commit a sin it becomes easier to do that sin again. Each time it gets a little easier. Until you are habitual NOT choosing to follow Christ. That is what sin is, an act of defiance or an act that breaks rules God set up.

Paul says, we should think about the meaning of our Baptism. When we are fully immersed into the water. We are buried in the death of Christ. In that the "dead are free from sin." In Baptism we are also brought up from the water, which speaks of Christ's resurrection. Being dead then resurrected as Christ should we not shun that which is sinful and live as Christ? Should we not choose that which is of God over that which is of the world? We should live for Christ! We should live lives wholly pleasing Christ our Lord, to honor Him who has chosen us to be His.

Dear Lord Jesus!

Lord, you offered me life in your death and resurrection. You set an example of how to live and more. Help me to make good choices. Help me to live as you would desire. Lead me to make those right decisions. Let my obedience to Your Word become that beacon on a hill that draws men unto you. For my righteousness is your righteousness. My salvation is because of nothing I did, Lord use me to let others see how great you are.

In Jesus name, Amen.

DAY #16
ROMANS 6:12-23
https://www.youtube.com/watch?v=k6_-wO7wSVI

12 Therefore do not let sin reign in your mortal body, that you should obey it in its lusts.

13 And do not present your members [as] instruments of unrighteousness to sin, but present yourselves to God as being alive from the dead, and your members [as] instruments of righteousness to God.

14 For sin shall not have dominion over you, for you are not under law but under grace.

15 What then? Shall we sin because we are not under law but under grace? Certainly not!

16 Do you not know that to whom you present yourselves slaves to obey, you are that one's slaves whom you obey, whether of sin [leading] to death, or of obedience [leading] to righteousness?

17 But God be thanked that [though] you were slaves of sin, yet you obeyed from the heart that form of doctrine to which you were delivered.

18 And having been set free from sin, you became slaves of righteousness.

19 I speak in human [terms] because of the weakness of your flesh. For just as you presented your members [as] slaves of uncleanness, and of lawlessness [leading] to [more] lawlessness, so now present your members [as] slaves [of] righteousness for holiness.

20 For when you were slaves of sin, you were free in regard to righteousness.

21 What fruit did you have then in the things of which you are now ashamed? For the end of those things [is] death.

22 But now having been set free from sin, and having become slaves of God, you have your fruit to holiness, and the end, everlasting life.

23 For the wages of sin [is] death, but the gift of God [is] eternal life in Christ Jesus our Lord.

To be HIS, to have made the choice to follow Him who saved you, to be one who recognized the glory and wonder in the work done on the cross by Christ Jesus is cause not to sin! Oh, it is true that there are some who say, "well, I am forgiven for my sins why shouldn't I sin more. God will forgive me anyways." But who is their real Master? Is it Christ, or the devil? After all the Word of God says, "it is not in man who walks to direct his steps" (Jeremiah 10:23).

What joy do we have knowing we were slaves of sin, but have been freed to become slaves of righteousness! What greater joy is there than knowing God has changed us so. Our actions are now fruit unto righteousness! We are not sinless, but we have one to whom to run to beg forgiveness for our sins. We have the great and almighty God who sought our salvation! We, though so unworthy, were bought with a price, that now we should become workers of righteousness. That alone by itself proves how worthy God is if worship, for we know who we were before we became HIS.

Dear Lord Jesus,

You have saved me from serving lusts, and desires that lead me towards hell. My works were piling up as dung. Lord, I am yours. Use me that I may share the joy you have granted me, to lead others to this great love You have shown me.

In Jesus name, Amen.

DAY #17
ROMANS 7:1-6
https://www.youtube.com/watch?v=k8QedcJZ7eY

1   Or do you not know, brethren (for I speak to those who know the law), that the law has dominion over a man as long as he lives?

2   For the woman who has a husband is bound by the law to [her] husband as long as he lives. But if the husband dies, she is released from the law of [her] husband.

3   So then if, while [her] husband lives, she marries another man, she will be called an adulteress; but if her husband dies, she is free from that law, so that she is no adulteress, though she has married another man.

4   Therefore, my brethren, you also have become dead to the law through the body of Christ, that you may be married to another--to Him who was raised from the dead, that we should bear fruit to God.

5	For when we were in the flesh, the sinful passions which were aroused by the law were at work in our members to bear fruit to death.
6	But now we have been delivered from the law, having died to what we were held by, so that we should serve in the newness of the Spirit and not [in] the oldness of the letter.

Sin – something we know of because of the law (Torah). The choice of words in verse 1 is truly interesting. We are under the "dominion," or "rule" of the law all our lives. We are "subject to" the law. We cannot escape it then, or can we? Law come with penalties for breaking them. They lack rewards. But the law is subject to the lawgiver. The very one who is over the law.

Knowing that we must receive the punishment that the law gives, Christ died for us. What then? His death paid our penalty. Then we as verse 4 have become dead to the law through the death of Christ. We were subject to our desires, we were in submission to sinful passions.

Christ not only made us dead from the law in his death, his resurrection grants us the ability to bear fruit unto God. Without this washing of our sins, what we do that is right is blackened by our sins. It is only in our acknowledgement of the wonder working power of Jesus sacrifice for our sins, that we receive the ability to do that which is good, free from the stain of sin. We owe so much to this glorious creator of ours.

Another way to look at this passage is to think of people who say they are going to heaven because of the good things (works) that they do. They may even brag about the good things they do for others. Romans 6 clearly tells us unless you are a Christian there is no way your good works are of any value to your salvation. As long as you carry the stain of sin your hard work towards doing the right thing is of no more value than a pile of dung.

Dear Lord Jesus,

Your wonder working power on the cross that saved a wretch like me, allows me to do good works and build up treasure in heaven. Lord, direct my path. Show me how I may honor you with good works. Lord, I beg of you to use me so that I may bear good fruit unto your glory.

In Jesus name, Amen.

DAY #18
ROMANS 7:7-25
https://www.youtube.com/watch?v=EK6vOvJIdvs

7 What shall we say then? [Is] the law sin? Certainly not! On the contrary, I would not have known sin except through the law. For I would not have known covetousness unless the law had said, "You shall not covet."

8 But sin, taking opportunity by the commandment, produced in me all [manner of evil] desire. For apart from the law sin [was] dead.

9 I was alive once without the law, but when the commandment came, sin revived and I died.

10 And the commandment, which [was] to [bring] life, I found to [bring] death.

11 For sin, taking occasion by the commandment, deceived me, and by it killed [me].

12 Therefore the law [is] holy, and the commandment holy and just and good.

13 Has then what is good become death to me? Certainly not! But sin, that it might appear sin, was producing death in me through what is good, so that sin through the commandment might become exceedingly sinful.

14 For we know that the law is spiritual, but I am carnal, sold under sin.

15 For what I am doing, I do not understand. For what I will to do, that I do not practice; but what I hate, that I do.

16 If, then, I do what I will not to do, I agree with the law that [it is] good.

17 But now, [it is] no longer I who do it, but sin that dwells in me.

18 For I know that in me (that is, in my flesh) nothing good dwells; for to will is present with me, but [how] to perform what is good I do not find.

19 For the good that I will [to do], I do not do; but the evil I will not [to do], that I practice.

20 Now if I do what I will not [to do], it is no longer I who do it, but sin that dwells in me.

21 I find then a law, that evil is present with me, the one who wills to do good.

22 For I delight in the law of God according to the inward man.

23 But I see another law in my members, warring against the law of my mind, and bringing me into captivity to the law of sin which is in my members.

24 O wretched man that I am! Who will deliver me from this body of death?

25   I thank God--through Jesus Christ our Lord! So then, with the mind I myself serve the law of God, but with the flesh the law of sin.

As believers we are in Christ, we more often than not know inwardly what is sin and what is not. Yet, we still often do that which we know should not. Paul here breaks down this struggle. Why is it that we commit sins? To think that without the law we could not be accused of sin, because we could not know we were sinning makes sins. But with that law we stand charged of the sins of we have committed. Yet, we who believe have a battle inside of ourselves. Our flesh has the desire to that which is sinful. Our mind can over rule our flesh and say to it, that is not pleasing to Christ. This war within ourselves can happen in milliseconds or days at a time.

Dear Lord Jesus!

You know our hearts and minds. You alone paid the price our sins have earned us. You alone have washed us free of our sins. Lord I give You praise for thinking of me. I give you praise for incredible love for me. Help me that I should share your love with the sheep who have yet to know you.

In Jesus name, Amen.

DAY #19
ROMANS 8:1
https://www.youtube.com/watch?v=qLk_s4P7Mzw

1   [There is] therefore now no condemnation to those who are in Christ Jesus, who do not walk according to the flesh, but according to the Spirit.

One of the reasons I love the King James Version is this verse. The NIV says, "Therefore, there is now no condemnation for those who are in Christ Jesus." The qualifier of this verse is missing! "Who do not walk according to the flesh but according to the Spirit" says who this verse speaks about. Oh, there are many who claim they follow Christ, and then do not live as He desires. Those who choose not live as Christ, give reason for there to be a condemnation against them. They do not live according to the Spirit but according to the flesh.

You are saved from the moment you accept Christ, you are not expected to make some miraculous change to who you are. But God works that change in you. Mankind is a creature of habit. We do not take to change easily. So, God works on our behaviors, our way of viewing life so that we may live according to the Spirit. God gives us fellowship with other believers to encourage us in living according to the Spirit. There is so much God does in us, to bring us to that place where we live according to the Spirit.

Christians are not perfect. They do make mistakes and allow the flesh to lead at times. They know these are acts of sin and there is condemnation then. They hear that in their heads. "Don't do that you know its wrong." "NO, make the other choice." "Crap, I knew I shouldn't have-----."

We have to make the choice to live as Christ, every day, every hour, every minute. We have to live according to the Spirit. The way to do that is what you are doing now. Daily reading of the Bible, feeding your spirit, the life breathing Word of God.

Dear Lord Jesus,

Thank you for being so personal to me. You gave us the Bible! Your Word feeds my spirit. It strengthens me to live for you! Help me to continue to live for you. Help me that I may be someone whose life draws others to live for you. Use me Lord. Use even my hum drum life to say to others, "his life is different. Why?" Let my life be that beacon on a hill.

In Jesus name, Amen.

DAY #20
ROMANS 8:2-17
https://youtu.be/l54tr40O9zo

2   For the law of the Spirit of life in Christ Jesus has made me free from the law of sin and death.

3   For what the law could not do in that it was weak through the flesh, God [did] by sending His own Son in the likeness of sinful flesh, on account of sin: He condemned sin in the flesh,

4   that the righteous requirement of the law might be fulfilled in us who do not walk according to the flesh but according to the Spirit.

5   For those who live according to the flesh set their minds on the things of the flesh, but those [who live] according to the Spirit, the things of the Spirit.

6   For to be carnally minded [is] death, but to be spiritually minded [is] life and peace.

7   Because the carnal mind [is] enmity against God; for it is not subject to the law of God, nor indeed can be.

8   So then, those who are in the flesh cannot please God.

9   But you are not in the flesh but in the Spirit, if indeed the Spirit of God dwells in you. Now if anyone does not have the Spirit of Christ, he is not His.

10   And if Christ [is] in you, the body [is] dead because of sin, but the Spirit [is] life because of righteousness.

11   But if the Spirit of Him who raised Jesus from the dead dwells in you, He who raised Christ from the dead will also give life to your mortal bodies through His Spirit who dwells in you.

12   Therefore, brethren, we are debtors--not to the flesh, to live according to the flesh.

13   For if you live according to the flesh you will die; but if by the Spirit you put to death the deeds of the body, you will live.

14   For as many as are led by the Spirit of God, these are sons of God.

15   For you did not receive the spirit of bondage again to fear, but you received the Spirit of adoption by whom we cry out, "Abba, Father."

16   The Spirit Himself bears witness with our spirit that we are children of God,

17   and if children, then heirs--heirs of God and joint heirs with Christ, if indeed we suffer with [Him], that we may also be glorified together.

The weakness of the law is that it points a finger at sin. Its solution is a continual stream of sacrifices for each and every person. Jesus fulfilled the Isaiah 53 prophecy and became the one true sacrifice for our sins. This act of a loving God had a few benefits beyond being a simple sacrifice for our sins.

Jesus death on the cross and his resurrection accompanied with a simple belief in His wonder working power grants us an ability to live according to the Spirit. For it is Christ who lives! He sent the Holy Spirit to us that we may live more abundantly.

The other benefit we receive is that we sinners, saved by the blood of Christ, not being bound by sin or fear, are now adopted.

To be adopted and called sons of God----is there a greater honor? Is there a greater gift? Truly we have a God worthy of worship above all others.

Dear Lord Jesus,

I praise you for your work on the cross. That one act of love has done more for me than I can even grasp. Lord, take this one you have adopted into called one of your own and use me. Use me that I may guide others to you. Help my life to beacon that shines of your glory calling the lost to you.

In Jesus name, Amen.

DAY #21
ROMANS 8:18-25
https://www.youtube.com/watch?v=eqHUZPjZpLs

18   For I consider that the sufferings of this present time are not worthy [to be compared] with the glory which shall be revealed in us.

19   For the earnest expectation of the creation eagerly waits for the revealing of the sons of God.

20   For the creation was subjected to futility, not willingly, but because of Him who subjected [it] in hope;

21   because the creation itself also will be delivered from the bondage of corruption into the glorious liberty of the children of God.

22   For we know that the whole creation groans and labors with birth pangs together until now.

23 Not only [that], but we also who have the first fruits of the Spirit, even we ourselves groan within ourselves, eagerly waiting for the adoption, the redemption of our body.

24 For we were saved in this hope, but hope that is seen is not hope; for why does one still hope for what he sees?

25 But if we hope for what we do not see, we eagerly wait for [it] with perseverance.

For many the world is a horrible place. Some live in the midst of a war torn country where death seems more real than the possibility of living to a ripe old age. Some people are fighting their own bodies for a chance to have it do what they want. Simple tasks like walking and eating can be taxing for them. It's a constant battle. While the world may seem horrible, we Christians have to remember our home is in heaven. Paul reminds us of the ever present reality our sufferings present to us cannot compare to that which is waiting for us! That everlasting life basked in a world filled with the presence of the God who loves us so!

Be ever mindful that this world's downfalls are nothing. We have HOPE! We have a promise by the SON OF GOD! We have the wonderworking power of His sacrifice that adopted us into being the sons of God. Even though we did nothing to deserve it.

Dear Lord Jesus!

You give us HOPE! You give us reason to fight on, to be free, to be more than we are, to make life better than it is, not only for ourselves, but for others. You alone are worthy of our worship. Use me Lord, Use me that I may draw others to see that glorious hope and promise in You.

In Jesus name, Amen.

DAY #22
ROMANS 8:26-27

https://www.youtube.com/watch?v=AgiFYhzPyJI

26   Likewise the Spirit also helps in our weaknesses. For we do not know what we should pray for as we ought, but the Spirit Himself makes intercession for us with groanings which cannot be uttered.

27   Now He who searches the hearts knows what the mind of the Spirit [is], because He makes intercession for the saints according to [the will of] God.

Have you ever been woken up in the middle of the night with an urge to pray for someone? How about you just feel something is wrong and start to pray? As Christians we sometimes find a compulsion to pray that we do not understand. We may not even know why we are praying or who we are praying for. This is one of those strange things that I have to admit to having had. For me it meant waking up at some weird time of night. I usually don't do this. So I took it as I need to pray. My son worked nights in the city as an EMT, so generally I prayed for him to have wisdom and for his safety. Another time I came out of an meeting for teachers at a school I did not work at and saw a gang of teens where I needed to the catch bus. I started to pray. Closed my eyes and asked God to send me a ride. Before I finished someone said, "Hey Paul, you need a ride?" To be honest I did not remember the person but they remembered me from a church I used to go to. I got in!

It's important for us to be obedient to these needs for prayer. God plans knowing he has given us choices, but when we listen and join in praying to him I like to think that changes things. Some might say it "turns things upside down," or "puts things right." All I know is that even though I simply might want to ignore that call to prayer, I need to do it.

Dear Lord Jesus,

May I listen to Your call for me to pray. May I not ignore your desires. Lead me into your righteousness. Lead me into seeking Your divine will. Use me Oh God, that I may share this great love you have for me and others.

In Jesus name, Amen.

DAY #23
ROMANS 8:28
https://www.youtube.com/watch?v=0hEnF1OyTpc

28 And we know that all things work together for good to them that love God, to them who are the called according to [his] purpose.

We may think we are in the midst of some incredible horrible tragedy. We may be bawling our eyes out, mourning, begging God for whatever to end, but God knows where we are and who we are at all times. Note that this verse is highly specific in who it is speaking about. It is speaking of Christians only.

Tragedies, horrible awful things, can only be put to good use through a God who loves us. He uses what is bad and sad in our lives. He wants you to accept Him as Lord of your life not only a part of you but all of you!

Some of the tragedies in my life led me to work in an area I never imagined myself in. I may have never had any interest if those tragedies never happened. How is God using the awful things that happened to you? Think about that and give Him the glory. Dietrich Bonhoeffer was captured by Hitler's men and scheduled to be executed. When the Allies were bombing the prisoners cowered in fear begging on God not kill them. But Bonhoeffer sat there calm. The peace of God overwhelmed him. This quiet silence of his during this horrible time was used to draw the lost to Christ.

As Christians we have hope in Jesus. We may feel overwhelmed with grief, fear, or horror. BUT we know Jesus is with us. We know He will carry us through even though we may feel incredibly weary. Then God will use this experience somehow for good.

Dear Lord Jesus,

You are the God who does impossible things. You take all of us and experiences and make us into something amazing – your joint heirs. Lord God, please mold me and make me after Your will. Use me that I may draw others unto you. Show me what I must do. Guide me. Never let me be away from Your love.

In Jesus Name. Amen.

DAY #24
ROMANS 8:29-32
https://www.youtube.com/watch?v=2jmKGsnPgW0

29   For whom He foreknew, He also predestined [to be] conformed to the image of His Son, that He might be the firstborn among many brethren.

30   Moreover whom He predestined, these He also called; whom He called, these He also justified; and whom He justified, these He also glorified.

31 What then shall we say to these things? If God [is] for us, who [can be] against us?

32 He who did not spare His own Son, but delivered Him up for us all, how shall He not with Him also freely give us all things?

One of the amazing wonders about this God who loves us so, is that he knew us before we were even thought of God was thinking of us! Yes we at some point made a choice to follow God. Vs. 29 says "He foreknew" not chose. God has all knowledge. He is not without knowledge of how and what we will do. He is such a God of love that he allows us to fall and make mistakes and pay the price for those things which we should not have done. Yet, because He, God knew we would choose Him, He made a way for us to join Him! The very act of love Christ gave in dying for us enabled us to be adopted as joint heirs. We were thus predestined, and are justified. We will also be glorified. When you have a God that loves you like this, what is there that can stand in your way? Who is it that can stand against you?

We serve a God who loves us beyond our comprehension. He sent the Bible to us piece by piece to communicate His love for us and wishes for us. So, yes! Yes! Who can stand against us when we have the all powerful God who loves us standing WITH US!

This does not mean we cannot die a physical death. It means, that we glory in it, because this is when we get to join our Lord in Heaven. But we live---we live to be that shining light of His. That beacon a hill that others may yet find Jesus!

Dear Lord Jesus!

Praise you! Praise you that you think so much of me. Praise you, for you alone are worthy of praise your love is not something we have to earn. It is not something we must slave for. It is freely given so that even when we were sinners you gave all that we may live. Lord use me. Use me that I may draw those who do not yet know your love to that overwhelming sense of joy in knowing you.

In Jesus name, Amen.

DAY #25
ROMANS 8:33-39
https://www.youtube.com/watch?v=lKOW3nyQ3sE

33   Who shall bring a charge against God's elect? [It is] God who justifies.

34   Who [is] he who condemns? [It is] Christ who died, and furthermore is also risen, who is even at the right hand of God, who also makes intercession for us.

35   Who shall separate us from the love of Christ? [Shall] tribulation, or distress, or persecution, or famine, or nakedness, or peril, or sword?

36   As it is written: "For Your sake we are killed all day long; We are accounted as sheep for the slaughter."

37   Yet in all these things we are more than conquerors through Him who loved us.

38   For I am persuaded that neither death nor life, nor angels nor principalities nor powers, nor things present nor things to come,

39   nor height nor depth, nor any other created thing, shall be able to separate us from the love of God which is in Christ Jesus our Lord.

It is important to understand that this passage is about your soul. Who shall dare to lay a charge against your soul when it is God who justifies. You may have indeed committed crimes in this world for which you must pay, but your soul has been redeemed! Who dares to do this? Who dares to accuse one who God has justified?

We know. Yes it is Satan. But there is also—You. All to often we commit some horrible sin, for which we cannot forgive ourselves even though we have asked God for forgiveness. We know that God forgives us, we believe it then after time passes we go back and think on this sin which we asked for forgiveness and feel the ton of guilt and shame as if it just happened. God took you into his arms just as you are. You didn't need to get all dressed up. You didn't need to work your way to a certain level of acceptance. You didn't need to burn off so many bad deeds by doing good ones for Him to come and embrace you with His love. He came to you because he loved you as a sinner. He loved you so much Christ offered His life as that living sacrifice for you! Think of God's love like this: When you ask God's forgiveness of a sin. He tosses that horrible stain of sin into a pool of water and then puts a sign up. "NO FISHING!"

Don't return to that sin. Learn what not to do. But do not return to the charge against your soul. Give praise to the God who loves you by doing that which is right in His eyes.

Dear Lord Jesus!

Your love – its like a mighty wave. Powerful, cleansing, and so much more! Praise YOU for having this love for even me. Lord, use me. Use me that I may share this incredible love You have given to me. Let me meekness, my shyness fall away, embolden me that I may share who You are and what You have done in my life with boldness.

In Jesus name, Amen.

DAY #26
ROMANS 9:1-13
https://www.youtube.com/watch?v=KPa53lTY0Kc

1   I tell the truth in Christ, I am not lying, my conscience also bearing me witness in the Holy Spirit,

2   that I have great sorrow and continual grief in my heart.

3   For I could wish that I myself were accursed from Christ for my brethren, my countrymen according to the flesh,

4   who are Israelites, to whom [pertain] the adoption, the glory, the covenants, the giving of the law, the service [of God], and the promises;

5   of whom [are] the fathers and from whom, according to the flesh, Christ [came], who is over all, [the] eternally blessed God. Amen.

6   But it is not that the word of God has taken no effect. For they [are] not all Israel who [are] of Israel,

7   nor [are they] all children because they are the seed of Abraham; but, "In Isaac your seed shall be called."

8   That is, those who [are] the children of the flesh, these [are] not the children of God; but the children of the promise are counted as the seed.

9   For this [is] the word of promise: "At this time I will come and Sarah shall have a son."

10   And not only [this], but when Rebecca also had conceived by one man, [even] by our father Isaac

11	(for [the children] not yet being born, nor having done any good or evil, that the purpose of God according to election might stand, not of works but of Him who calls),
12	it was said to her, "The older shall serve the younger."
13	As it is written, "Jacob I have loved, but Esau I have hated."

Paul, a Jew feels pain in his heart because he like so many others prided themselves on being God's chosen nation. They believe they are the very elect by birth. Paul here says, yes, they are the chosen nation. Yes, they are God's Chosen people. BUT they are not the elect who are only that. God's grace is for those who choose to follow Him and not only for the Jews. Paul understands that Jesus came to save the lost. That His message for exceeds anything before. This message that fulfills so many promises of God. This message of love and sacrifice goes even beyond His chosen people! Is given to those who have faith. For Paul this is message is drastically important as it reaches far beyond His own people. Yet, it is His own, God's Chosen who eject Paul and the Gospel message he shares. They do so and place their faith in God and thank God for their birth. They think of their birth as what saves them, not the wonder working power of the blood of Christ.

Dear Lord Jesus!

I may not come from much. My birth gives me no place of authority, nor rights. You alone did this marvelous work that has saved me. Lord use me to share this over powering love that saves all who simply believe.

In Jesus name, Amen.

50 DAYS IN ROMANS

DAY #27
ROMANS 9:14-21
https://www.youtube.com/watch?v=T0T1NSLO3L0

14   What shall we say then? [Is there] unrighteousness with God? Certainly not!

15   For He says to Moses, "I will have mercy on whomever I will have mercy, and I will have compassion on whomever I will have compassion."

16   So then [it is] not of him who wills, nor of him who runs, but of God who shows mercy.

17   For the Scripture says to the Pharaoh, "For this very purpose I have raised you up, that I may show My power in you, and that My name may be declared in all the earth."

18   Therefore He has mercy on whom He wills, and whom He wills He hardens.

19   You will say to me then, "Why does He still find fault? For who has resisted His will?"

20   But indeed, O man, who are you to reply against God? Will the thing formed say to him who formed [it], "Why have you made me like this?"

21   Does not the potter have power over the clay, from the same lump to make one vessel for honor and another for dishonor?

"GOD DON"T MAKE JUNK!" Many years ago, I heard a person talk on this and how gloriously and wonderfully you and I were made. You may have something that does not seem perfect about your body, you may be to heavy, or too skinny. You may have some deformity or a cancer. You may have a learning disability. I do. Even so God formed you! He knew what he was doing when he made you. You may have difficulty walking, or talking. God made you this way for a reason. It is still our job to give them God made you! Better he chose you to be His own. This God of Love made us with His own hands. You are HIS creation. To have been personally molded by great and powerful God tells us we should honor all life.

Dear Lord Jesus!

Thank you for making me who I am. Your hand has guided me, carried me and more through the journey of life. Lord help me to continue to strive to do your will. Help me that I may make the right choices not ones that fulfill my own selfish desires. Use me Lord, use that I may show others this great and glorious love you have for us!

In Jesus name, Amen.

DAY #28
ROMANS 9:22-33

https://www.youtube.com/watch?v=SupbjNP9q44

22   [What] if God, wanting to show [His] wrath and to make His power known, endured with much longsuffering the vessels of wrath prepared for destruction,

23   and that He might make known the riches of His glory on the vessels of mercy, which He had prepared beforehand for glory,

24   even us whom He called, not of the Jews only, but also of the Gentiles?

25	As He says also in Hosea: "I will call them My people, who were not My people, And her beloved, who was not beloved."
26	"And it shall come to pass in the place where it was said to them, 'You [are] not My people,' There they shall be called sons of the living God."
27	Isaiah also cries out concerning Israel: "Though the number of the children of Israel be as the sand of the sea, The remnant will be saved.
28	For He will finish the work and cut [it] short in righteousness, Because the LORD will make a short work upon the earth."
29	And as Isaiah said before: "Unless the LORD of Sabaoth had left us a seed, We would have become like Sodom, And we would have been made like Gomorrah."
30	What shall we say then? That Gentiles, who did not pursue righteousness, have attained to righteousness, even the righteousness of faith;
31	but Israel, pursuing the law of righteousness, has not attained to the law of righteousness.
32	Why? Because [they did] not [seek it] by faith, but as it were, by the works of the law. For they stumbled at that stumbling stone.
33	As it is written: "Behold, I lay in Zion a stumbling stone and rock of offense, And whoever believes on Him will not be put to shame."

Paul here shows his knowledge as a rabbi. He shares the very real truth that salvation from God goes beyond the Jewish people and they should know it! The rabbis knew of the coming of Jesus and they understood that a message of salvation was coming that would grab the heart of Gentiles as well. It almost seems as if he has to justify salvation to the Gentiles to the Roman church. This reveals that a good many of them may have been Jews, and those that were Jews may have felt a sense of superiority also. The cited verses here reveal the Jews have only survived because of the promise of God. Yes, they are indeed the chosen people, but their own actions have created stumbling blocks to salvation in Christ Jesus. It is only through His grace any of us has salvation. Paul clearly laid that out in previous chapters. We are all unworthy. Even His chosen people are unworthy.

Precious Lord Jesus,

Thank you that you saved a wretch like me. For I am truly only Yours because of your incredible love. Lord, please work on me. Mold me that I may share Your love with others. Use this wretched person to share your great love. Use me that I may share my joy in Your salvation of this person who so needs your love.

In Jesus name, Amen.

DAY #29
ROMANS 10:1-4
https://www.youtube.com/watch?v=LAi2BSDa2FA

1   Brethren, my heart's desire and prayer to God for Israel is, that they might be saved.

2   For I bear them record that they have a zeal of God, but not according to knowledge.

3	For they being ignorant of God's righteousness, and going about to establish their own righteousness, have not submitted themselves unto the righteousness of God.
4	For Christ [is] the end of the law for righteousness to every one that believes.

Paul's heart is for those of his own, fellow Jews. He talks about their zeal and their ignorance. This reminds me of my encounters with people who believe their good works will earn them a place in heaven. It's a sad conversation. They are zealous at doing what they believe is good. They help old ladies with their groceries. Run to help others constantly, figuring that all these good deeds create good Karma—a force for good that will earn them a place in heaven. Their intentions in doing good is building up earnings to the right spot in the afterlife. Yet, when you talk about sin, they shy away and sometimes runaway. Why? Because to discuss sin is to discuss what is right by God's standards, not that of men. This is not an easy discussion for anyone simply because we all have sinned. No one likes to think about things they have done that deserve some form of punishment. Some things bring shame and disgust. Some sins make us wonder can we do more good deeds to cover up that sin I did. The answer is NO. Nothing we can do will save us. Jesus did everything for. We only need to believe in his sacrifice his work on the cross for us. We can't earn a thing towards heaven.

Dear Lord Jesus!

Thank you for making it impossible for me to earn my way to heaven. I probably would never have found my way. It is as your Word says, While we were yet sinners, you died for us. You did not wait for my sins to bring me to repentance. You did this all before I even knew. Lord, thank you and praise you for loving even me. Use me that I may share your great with others.

In Jesus name, Amen.

DAY #30
ROMANS 10:5-13
https://www.youtube.com/watch?v=cqvs6GH_5z8

5 For Moses describes the righteousness which is of the law, That the man which does those things shall live by them.

6 But the righteousness which is of faith speaks on this wise, Say not in your heart, Who shall ascend into heaven? (that is, to bring Christ down [from above]:)

7 Or, Who shall descend into the deep? (that is, to bring up Christ again from the dead.)

8 But what saith it? The word is nigh you, [even] in your mouth, and in your heart: that is, the word of faith, which we preach;

9 That if you shalt confess with your mouth the Lord Jesus, and shalt believe in your heart that God hath raised him from the dead, you shalt be saved.

10 For with the heart man believes unto righteousness; and with the mouth confession is made unto salvation.

11 For the scripture says, Whosoever believes on him shall not be ashamed.

12 For there is no difference between the Jew and the Greek: for the same Lord over all is rich unto all that call upon him.

13 For whosoever shall call upon the name of the Lord shall be saved.

Here you have it. As simple as it gets—the truth about how to be saved. The entire list of requirements. Do you see list? I only count one thing. There is no special requirement! All you have to do is believe in your heart. God comes to you where you are at. It really is that simple. Some people want you to be just so. But Jesus ONLY WANTS YOU AS YOU ARE!

Dear Lord Jesus!

Thank you for seeking me out. You knocked and I finally answered on that day. Mold me, for I am yours. Use me as I am Yours.

In Jesus name, Amen.

DAY #31
ROMANS 10:14-15
https://www.youtube.com/watch?v=cIYCHzvCHF0

14   How then shall they call on him in whom they have not believed? and how shall they believe in him of whom they have not heard? and how shall they hear without a preacher?

15   And how shall they preach, except they be sent? as it is written, How beautiful are the feet of them that preach the gospel of peace, and bring glad tidings of good things!

Our responsibility as Christians to share God's Word has never been more important than it is today. How shall they hear of Jesus unless you and I share about him. We need to share Jesus in our words and deeds. We need to be that good neighbor. We need to be that friend who is there when we are needed. We need to give time, and effort to sharing Jesus. We need to be out there.

The world is very different today than the world I was born into 50 some years ago. As I was growing up I don't think I knew of anyone who did not know who Jesus is. Some had wrong ideas, but everyone knew who Jesus is. As a teacher I met numerous students who had no clue who Jesus is. They had no understanding why people would go to church, nor why anyone should pray. This world is ripe for a harvest. It needs to hear about Christ! So you and I are needed to share Jesus! I guess that makes all of us preachers of the good news. We are sent by God to all the earth. We are sent by our fellow Christians to share with others.

It's not our words that are marvelous and beautiful when sharing Christ. It is our feet for having gone where the Lord has sent us to share the Gospel message. That is because we but plant seeds. He is Lord of the harvest. They get to hear about Jesus from our words and deeds. Our words are not flowery. We speak of sin and the need for salvation. Our feet are beautiful.

Dear Lord Jesus!

Oh Great and glorious God!

Mold me and make me after your will that I may share Your word. That I may be used to share the Good News of your work on the cross for us. Send me that I may speak the right words so that someone may make that choice to follow You!

In Jesus name, Amen.

DAY #32
ROMANS 10:16-21
https://www.youtube.com/watch?v=4SiuC9IcBSE

16   But they have not all obeyed the gospel. For Esaias saith, Lord, who hath believed our report?

17   So then faith [comes] by hearing, and hearing by the word of God.

18   But I say, Have they not heard? Yes verily, their sound went into all the earth, and their words unto the ends of the world.

19   But I say, Did not Israel know? First Moses saith, I will provoke you to jealousy by [them that are] no people, [and] by a foolish nation I will anger you.

20   But Esaias is very bold, and saith, I was found of them that sought me not; I was made manifest unto them that asked not after me.

21   But to Israel he saith, All day long I have stretched forth my hands unto a disobedient and gainsaying people.

Even though God has sent people to preach the good news of the wonderworking power of Jesus blood shed for them, some still do not believe. This means they have been disobedient to the good news. We should react and be thankful for what God has done for us.

What's interesting in the next verse is how. How the gospel is to be preached is key. It must be through the preaching of His Word. You can share the good news of the death and resurrection of Jesus, but for it to be effective we must share God's Word – the Bible! We must give much more attention to memorizing scripture. We must embed God's word in our life to get the message of His love out.

The Jewish people had the law (Torah), the prophets (Naveem) and the writings (Keth-ub-eem) and they had heard it so often it became ingrained in them. So what reason do they have for not believing in the Messiah God sent to them? Paul says they are disobedient to the Good News. Pau, the good rabbi, share with us scriptures that show God foretold of this. He knew this and shared it with His chosen people the Jews. But still his hand is stretched out to them.

We must become concerned about those who do not know Christ. We must take it upon ourselves to share His love with them. We must live in such a way that they ask why our lives are different and seem better. We must fill ourselves with God's Word in case an opportunity arises to share (preach) who Christ is and what he has done for us.

Dear Lord Jesus,

You offer us so much. You watch over us and keep us safe. Lord help me to place Your Word in my heart. Help me to not only memorize it so that I may live it, but help me to keep it in my heart so that I may share Your love with others. Prepare me Lord, that I may be used of You to share Your Word.

In Jesus name, Amen.

DAY #33
ROMANS 11:1-10
https://www.youtube.com/watch?v=_8n6zj-b9C4

1   I say then, has God cast away His people? Certainly not! For I also am an Israelite, of the seed of Abraham, [of] the tribe of Benjamin.

2   God has not cast away His people whom He foreknew. Or do you not know what the Scripture says of Elijah, how he pleads with God against Israel, saying,

3	*"LORD, they have killed Your prophets and torn down Your altars, and I alone am left, and they seek my life"?*
4	But what does the divine response say to him? *"I have reserved for Myself seven thousand men who have not bowed the knee to Baal."*
5	Even so then, at this present time there is a remnant according to the election of grace.
6	And if by grace, then [it is] no longer of works; otherwise grace is no longer grace. But if [it is] of works, it is no longer grace; otherwise work is no longer work.
7	What then? Israel has not obtained what it seeks; but the elect have obtained it, and the rest were blinded.
8	Just as it is written: *"God has given them a spirit of stupor, Eyes that they should not see And ears that they should not hear, To this very day."*
9	And David says: *"Let their table become a snare and a trap, A stumbling block and a recompense to them.*
10	*Let their eyes be darkened, so that they do not see, And bow down their back always."*

Paul had to be pondering why the Jews would not be easily receptive to the good news of Jesus their Messiah. Being Jewish the disciples went to the Jews first to spread the Good News. He had to be pondering why, he also was filled with hatred, and blinded to the truth of the Gospel until Jesus met him on the road to Damascus. In this passage you can almost hear him crying out to God, "Why Lord, why have we not seen the light in the truth of what You have done for us. Why is it not easier for us to see the fulfillment of scripture?" Scripture gives the answer. The question was answered before Paul even asked it. There were multiple passages on this!

> Isaiah 29:10
> *For the LORD has poured out on you The spirit of deep sleep, And has closed your eyes, namely, the prophets; And He has covered your heads, [namely], the seers.*

> Deuteronomy 29:4
> *"Yet the LORD has not given you a heart to perceive and eyes to see and ears to hear, to this [very] day.*

> Isaiah 6:9]
> *And He said, "Go, and tell this people: 'Keep on hearing, but do not understand; Keep on seeing, but do not perceive.'*

> Jeremiah 5:21
> *'Hear this now, O foolish people, Without understanding, Who have eyes and see not, And who have ears and hear not:*

> Ezekiel 12:2
> *"Son of man, you dwell in the midst of a rebellious house, which has eyes to see but does not see, and ears to hear but does not hear; for they [are] a rebellious house.*

Dear Lord Jesus,

You answer our questions before we even know them. We feel lost, but you are the Good Shepherd. You searched for us until we were found. You won't let us go. Your love for us knows no bounds. It is far above our own ability to love. It is a reason to give You glory! Use me Lord, that I may share this wondrous love you have for us. Use me that I may shine a light directing others to find You as the answer they seek.

In Jesus name, Amen.

DAY #34
ROMANS 11:11-24
https://www.youtube.com/watch?v=cOE4q3flaBA

11 I say then, have they stumbled that they should fall? Certainly not! But through their fall, to provoke them to jealousy, salvation [has come] to the Gentiles.

12 Now if their fall [is] riches for the world, and their failure riches for the Gentiles, how much more their fullness!

13 For I speak to you Gentiles; inasmuch as I am an apostle to the Gentiles, I magnify my ministry,

14 if by any means I may provoke to jealousy [those who are] my flesh and save some of them.

15 For if their being cast away [is] the reconciling of the world, what [will] their acceptance [be] but life from the dead?

16 For if the firstfruit [is] holy, the lump [is] also [holy]; and if the root [is] holy, so [are] the branches.

17 And if some of the branches were broken off, and you, being a wild olive tree, were grafted in among them, and with them became a partaker of the root and fatness of the olive tree,

18 do not boast against the branches. But if you do boast, [remember that] you do not support the root, but the root [supports] you.

19	You will say then, "Branches were broken off that I might be grafted in."
20	Well [said]. Because of unbelief they were broken off, and you stand by faith. Do not be haughty, but fear.
21	For if God did not spare the natural branches, He may not spare you either.
22	Therefore consider the goodness and severity of God: on those who fell, severity; but toward you, goodness, if you continue in [His] goodness. Otherwise you also will be cut off.
23	And they also, if they do not continue in unbelief, will be grafted in, for God is able to graft them in again.
24	For if you were cut out of the olive tree which is wild by nature, and were grafted contrary to nature into a cultivated olive tree, how much more will these, who [are] natural [branches], be grafted into their own olive tree?

Paul continues to talk about the Jews here. They lost faith, their refusal the Good News of Jesus separates them from the Love or Christ. In their place we, the Gentiles (non Jews) are grafted into the "family tree." We should keep in mind that the He is the Vine. He is the one whose wondrous work allows us to be accepted into the Kingdom of God. We have no reason to think of ourselves as great high and mighty for it is of nothing that we did that we get such a reward. Then there is nothing – nothing that should let us Lord over others our salvation. This incredible work of Christ was done for all. But how much more natural it must be that a Jewish person finds Jesus. Everything they have learned and been taught all their lives becomes clearer. They see the scriptures fulfilled! We must continue to pray for the Jewish people that they would find the Messiah who came and died for them.

Dear Lord Jesus,

You have done so much to be worthy of my praise and prayers. Lord, I ask that You teach me what I need to know to reach the Jewish people for you. Use me that I may bring the lost to you. Guide me, that I may plant seeds of Your Word amongst the lost, that they may find Your love for them. Praise be to You oh Lord, the only Wise King!

In Jesus name, Amen.

DAY #35
ROMANS 11:25-36

https://www.youtube.com/watch?v=Hac5h_CejBA

25 For I do not desire, brethren, that you should be ignorant of this mystery, lest you should be wise in your own opinion, that blindness in part has happened to Israel until the fullness of the Gentiles has come in.

26 And so all Israel will be saved, as it is written: "The Deliverer will come out of Zion, And He will turn away ungodliness from Jacob;

27 For this [is] My covenant with them, When I take away their sins."

28 Concerning the gospel [they are] enemies for your sake, but concerning the election [they are] beloved for the sake of the fathers.

29 For the gifts and the calling of God [are] irrevocable.

30 For as you were once disobedient to God, yet have now obtained mercy through their disobedience,

31   even so these also have now been disobedient, that through the mercy shown you they also may obtain mercy.

32   For God has committed them all to disobedience, that He might have mercy on all.

33   Oh, the depth of the riches both of the wisdom and knowledge of God! How unsearchable [are] His judgments and His ways past finding out!

34   "For who has known the mind of the LORD? Or who has become His counselor?"

35   "Or who has first given to Him And it shall be repaid to him?"

36   For of Him and through Him and to Him [are] all things, to whom [be] glory forever. Amen.

To think that we can have an answer to what is going on when Jews reject their Messiah, yet still have a promise that they are the Chosen people may seem silly. Yet here Paul lays out the answer simply. Their loss is the gain of the world. It allowed us to be grafted into the vine. BUT God has not and will not abandon them. They still have prophecies of promise to them. God is above us. God needs no counsel. He alone is the cause of all things. To Him alone belongs our praise!

Dear Lord Jesus,

You give us knowledge, answer our Christians with noes and yesses. Even though we do not often like your answers. Lord we owe You everything and often say and do little to show how we love You. Work on me God, that I may praise You even during tough times. Work on me that I may become Your instrument of praise. Use me then that I may share your glory with others.

In Jesus name, Amen.

DAY #36
ROMANS 12:1-2
https://www.youtube.com/watch?v=guPp5Opw7j4

1   I beseech you therefore, brethren, by the mercies of God, that you present your bodies a living sacrifice, holy, acceptable unto God, [which is] your reasonable service.

2   And be not conformed to this world: but be you transformed by the renewing of your mind, that you may prove what [is] that good, and acceptable, and perfect, will of God.

Your bodies are the temple of God. How you treat it, what you put into it, how you spend your time and much more effect make your temple of God able to withstand the temptations placed before you by the enemy. Each of us is uniquely made by God, we each have our quirks, our own desires for good and temptations that if we give in bring us down. One thing that is true about presenting your body as a living sacrifice is that the more often you stand up and do what is right vs. giving into temptation, the easier it gets to withstand that temptation. Saying no to something at first can be struggle if you were addicted. But after saying no a second time, 10th, time, and 144th time is different. Practice doing what God wants of you makes your body a living sacrifice. It does not mean you do harm to yourself, buy you live as an example of Christ!

The renewing of your mind is intertwined with making your body a living sacrifice. Think on those things that are Good and just and of God, learning Scripture, memorizing it, and sometimes simply saying no are all steps and tools to the renewing of you mind.

Without these two things, the renewing of your mind, and placing your body as a living sacrifice you cannot be effective as an example of Jesus. Yet this is what we desire as Christians.

Dear Lord Jesus!

Without you – I have nothing. Your all-powerful, incredibly loving grace for me is what I needed even before I understood that need. Lord continue to mold and shape me after Your will. Help me that I may more perfectly reflect Your love for others.

In Jesus name. Amen.

DAY #37
ROMANS 12:3-8
https://www.youtube.com/watch?v=rhusWDSLq_Y

3   For I say, through the grace given unto me, to every man that is among you, not to think [of himself] more highly than he ought to think; but to think soberly, according as God hath dealt to every man the measure of faith.

4   For as we have many members in one body, and all members have not the same office:

5   So we, [being] many, are one body in Christ, and every one members one of another.

6   Having then gifts differing according to the grace that is given to us, whether prophecy, [let us prophesy] according to the proportion of faith;

7   Or ministry, [let us wait] on [our] ministering: or he that teaches, on teaching;

8   Or he that exhorts, on exhortation: he that gives, [let him do it] with simplicity; he that rules, with diligence; he that shows mercy, with cheerfulness.

While we are the elect of God, the ones God chose to bestow his grace, we are each but one person. Being the elect of God does not make us God. We need to rely on the knowledge that God gave each of talents. But not the same talents to everyone. You may be a great writer, another a great artist as a drawer, yet another a master of color. If the three elect work together they may create a bold evangelical cartoon calling the lost to Christ.

Our talents are different! They make us stand out within our own community of believers. They make our ministry to the brethren and to the lost unique. God LOVES that uniqueness in each of us. He celebrates it! God uses this to teach us as a whole about ourselves comparing us to how our body works, and how that uniqueness in the individual makes the body work as a unit. The person called of God to lead a flock of believers may be highly talented reaching each and everyone of his flock, teaching them well about the Word, but he may know nothing of plumbing.

Even so are the gifts of God different. Not everyone can teach, some are great as Mentors (exhorters), they help you grow and encourage you every step of the way. Another way of viewing this is to recognize our own limitations. If your gift of God is in one area, and you truly need help or advice from someone who has another gift, seek it! There is nothing wrong with admitting God made you who you are and recognizing and celebrating that difference by asking for help from another.

God even reminds us that our gifts are simply that -- Gifts from God. We have no right to think of ourselves as better because we have certain gifts.

Dear Lord Jesus!

Work on me. Mold me after Your will. Stop me from allowing my pride to lift me up. Let me remember You gave each of us special gifts. I am but one of your servants. Bind me with others that my gifts from you may shine. That their gifts also might shine. Lord use us as whole that we may share Your great love and mercy in a new way that draws many to you.

In Jesus name, Amen.

DAY #38
ROMANS 12:9-21
https://www.youtube.com/watch?v=CA44V1zlyAg

9   [Let] love be without dissimulation. Abhor that which is evil; cleave to that which is good.

10   [Be] kindly affectioned one to another with brotherly love; in honour preferring one another;

11   Not slothful in business; fervent in spirit; serving the Lord;

12   Rejoicing in hope; patient in tribulation; continuing instant in prayer;

13   Distributing to the necessity of saints; given to hospitality.

14   Bless them which persecute you: bless, and curse not.

15   Rejoice with them that do rejoice, and weep with them that weep.

16   [Be] of the same mind one toward another. Mind not high things, but condescend to men of low estate. Be not wise in your own conceits.

17   Recompense to no man evil for evil. Provide things honest in the sight of all men.

18	If it be possible, as much as lies in you, live peaceably with all men.
19	Dearly beloved, avenge not yourselves, but [rather] give place unto wrath: for it is written, Vengeance [is] mine; I will repay, saith the Lord.
20	Therefore if your enemy hunger, feed him; if he thirst, give him drink: for in so doing you shalt heap coals of fire on his head.
21	Be not overcome of evil, but overcome evil with good.

In a pagan society, a place without any understanding of who God is, these rules for living may have seemed weird, strange even. Don't return evil for evil may have seemed foreign. Once while talking to a friend he talked about the rules of the street vs. how God wanted us to act. He spoke of how you never turn your back an enemy because that is when they strike. Taking the turning of the back as an insult, as if they were not a significant threat. His back against the wall later in life as he preached, he felt the need and importance to not return evil for evil. He did turn his back to someone but it wasn't to insult, it was to place confidence in God who has his back. HE closed his eyes expecting a beating. Instead something beautiful happened. A seed was planted of love, because he did not treat the other person as a threat. You never know how doing what is of God can effect those around who may be simply watching thinking they will see you fall. Returning Good for Evil – it may seem like an opposite world reaction, but think of Christ as he was found in the garden the last night he had on earth. Peter drew his sword to act as Jesus' protector. He faced the soldier and cut off his ear. What did Jesus do? Did he call his men to fight? No, instead he healed that man's ear. What must he have thought of the man he brought before the Jewish council.

Dear Lord Jesus,

Help me to think before I act and react. Help me to not express anger but love. Help me to seek Your wisdom and knowledge. Help me to return a smile for a slap. Help me Lord that I may stand as an example of you! Let me testimony be a living testament of Your love.

In Jesus name, Amen.

DAY #39
ROMANS 13:1-7
https://www.youtube.com/watch?v=G6-0Dcp6o2g

1   Let every soul be subject unto the higher powers. For there is no power but of God: the powers that be are ordained of God.

2   Whosoever therefore resists the power, resists the ordinance of God: and they that resist shall receive to themselves damnation.

3   For rulers are not a terror to good works, but to the evil. Wilt you then not be afraid of the power? do that which is good, and you shalt have praise of the same:

4   For he is the minister of God to you for good. But if you do that which is evil, be afraid; for he bears not the sword in vain: for he is the minister of God, a revenger to [execute] wrath upon him that does evil.

5   Wherefore [you] must needs be subject, not only for wrath, but also for conscience sake.

6   For this cause pay your tribute also: for they are God's ministers, attending continually upon this very thing.

7   Render therefore to all their dues: tribute to whom tribute [is due]; custom to whom custom; fear to whom fear; honour to whom honour.

One of the things that sets Christianity apart from most other religions is the teaching that we should submit to the governing entity wherever we live. We should still give respect to it, paying our taxes, and doing that which is good. While there are times we as Christians must stand up as soldiers and resist a government entity whose actions are that of evil, like Hitler's reign in Germany and more, in most cases, we should submit as good subjects. Verse 3 here is that defining edge of when should we not submit. When the government is a terror to good works, then we should be actively acting against the government. In a nutshell that means the day crime is rewarded and those that seek to fight crime are jailed.

Christians are to pray for those in leadership roles over them. We should keep our pastors, our teachers, our law enforcement, our mayors, and other government representatives such as our president in our prayers daily. This is how we can best assist those serving in government roles. Asking God to strengthen and use them has to be a daily priority.

There are some out there who resist paying taxes. In truth, none of us wants to pay taxes. We hate it. But this is an imperative from Christ. We need to pay our taxes as a way to submit to the government God has placed over us.

Dear Lord Jesus,

Work on me, and help me never to forget praying for those over me. Help me to honor You Lord, I pray for Pastor_____, and for Mayor____, for President____ that they would be blessed of you. Lord direct their footsteps and lead them to do mighty works for

You. Help me Lord, that in my honoring Your will I may be an example that leads others to know of Your love.

In Jesus name, Amen.

DAY #40
ROMANS 13:8-10
https://www.youtube.com/watch?v=NW-a-au5jcY

8   Owe no man any thing, but to love one another: for he that loves another has fulfilled the law.

9   For this, You shalt not commit adultery, You shalt not kill, You shalt not steal, You shalt not bear false witness, You shalt not covet; and if [there be] any other commandment, it is briefly comprehended in this saying, namely, You shalt love your neighbour as yourself.

10 Love works no ill to his neighbour: therefore love [is] the fulfilling of the law.

A few years back a friend from church started a Bible study. It was great. Herb, ran the club starting off with prayer and then sharing what he called Friendship evangelism events and what we jokingly called Starbucks evangelism. Herb met people and struck up conversations getting to know them personally over time. Many got to know him as that Jesus lover. But Herb did not press. He simply waited until opportunity arose. Some of his stories talked of being there when no one else seemed to be. Just being there can have the greatest impact. Just listening. Allowing the neighbor or acquaintance to vent, cry, share can reach deeper than we can ever know. Who do you think of when you imagine someone just being there for you? My bet is that it is not someone who breaks commandments. It is the person who sat by your hospital bed when you were in such pain conversation was hard. Maybe it's the person who was there to listen to you cry out after some horrible event. We as Christians have a duty to share the Gospel. In America, there is a social stigma against those who share the Good News of Jesus in social gatherings. But is there for one who does this in private after being that example of friendship. After being the one who listens and is there for them in their time of need do you think they will not listen to you? We have to live and breathe as examples of Christ, and be good examples of friendship. That earns us a stage to share what brings us joy and hope – our Messiah, our God, JESUS! Don't miss those opportunities to build up that stage.

Dear Lord Jesus,

Work on us and make us examples to others. Mold us that we may be there for others in their time of need. Help us to listen and think of the power of your love. Help us to be there whenever we can, with whatever talent you have given us to help others. Use us to share your love by friendship, and any way possible so that others may learn what excites us about You. You first loved us!

In Jesus name, Amen.

DAY #41
ROMANS 13:11-14
https://www.youtube.com/watch?v=-tk4nRLrZeA

11   And that, knowing the time, that now [it is] high time to awake out of sleep: for now [is] our salvation nearer than when we believed.

12	The night is far spent, the day is at hand: let us therefore cast off the works of darkness, and let us put on the armour of light.
13	Let us walk honestly, as in the day; not in rioting and drunkenness, not in sexual immorality and wantonness, not in strife and envying.
14	But put on the Lord Jesus Christ, and make not provision for the flesh, to [fulfil] the lusts [thereof].

We are in the last days. Jesus is coming soon. Will we be ready? Will we have shared His name and been part of someone coming to Christ? Will we have been examples of living as Christ desires instead of living in lust? Will we have been someone's example of what it means to be a Christian?

In today's topsy turvy world, people rarely hold back from drinking too much and expressing their lustful desires. We see this on display online and sadly, often in public. Is this the example we want to be to others? We need to be examples of living right before God, not examples of how easy it is to live and fulfill our lusts.

None of us knows when Christ will return. Oh we might guess at the times but we can not know. We have to live as if Jesus is coming back in the next hour. We have to live as if HIS return is any second. Would you do anything different? Maybe clean more? Maybe choose your words with more care? Live for HIM.

Dear Lord Jesus,

Mold me and make me after your will. Make me seek after your desires not my own. Help me to choose that which is right so I may be a better example of who You are. Lord I ask that you would use me to draw others to finding You.

In Jesus name, Amen.

DAY #42
ROMANS 14:1
https://www.youtube.com/watch?v=E2Tx7_HK7j4

1   Him that is weak in the faith receive you, [but] not to doubtful disputations.

This verse has an interesting profound importance, that is illustrated in the rest of the chapter. It means "to take in your younger weaker believers," for the encouraging of growth in the Scriptures. It is so important to do this to encourage new believers, but not to dispute or argue with their thoughts. Some things must be left to God to work on. A person's thoughts are not doctrine and do not need correction. Thoughts are not actions. Why condemn someone for something they have never done only thought about.

As a believer I have seen some people argue over things that seem unnecessary to debate. Younger, weaker members of a faith see this and question what is going on the wander wondering how judgmental can a Christian be? Arguments like this make not just one stumble but those around listening.

Dear Lord Jesus,

I thank you that you are here, loving me. Helping me to grow in Your Word. Help me to be an example of how to live for You. Help me to seek you out first and foremost above all. Do not let me argue about useless things. Lord, use me that I may encourage people weak in the faith. Use me that I may help their growth. Embolden me that I may share

In Jesus name, Amen.

DAY #43
ROMANS 14:2-23
https://www.youtube.com/watch?v=vew5z5nQ11g

2   For one believes that he may eat all things: another, who is weak, eats herbs.

3   Let not him that eats despise him that eats not; and let not him which eats not judge him that eats: for God hath received him.

4   Who art you that judges another man's servant? to his own master he stands or falls. Yea, he shall be holden up: for God is able to make him stand.

5   One man esteems one day above another: another esteems every day [alike]. Let every man be fully persuaded in his own mind.

6   He that regards the day, regards [it] unto the Lord; and he that regards not the day, to the Lord he doth not regard [it]. He that eats, eats to the Lord, for he gives God thanks; and he that eats not, to the Lord he eats not, and gives God thanks.

7   For none of us lives to himself, and no man dies to himself.

8   For whether we live, we live unto the Lord; and whether we die, we die unto the Lord: whether we live therefore, or die, we are the Lord's.

9   For to this end Christ both died, and rose, and revived, that he might be Lord both of the dead and living.

10 But why do you judge your brother? or why do you set at nought your brother? for we shall all stand before the judgment seat of Christ.

11   For it is written, [As] I live, saith the Lord, every knee shall bow to me, and every tongue shall confess to God.

12   So then every one of us shall give account of himself to God.

13   Let us not therefore judge one another any more: but judge this rather, that no man put a stumbling block or an occasion to fall in [his] brother's way.

14   I know, and am persuaded by the Lord Jesus, that [there is] nothing unclean of itself: but to him that esteems any thing to be unclean, to him [it is] unclean.

15   But if your brother be grieved with [your] meat, now walk you not charitably. Destroy not him with your meat, for whom Christ died.

16   Let not then your good be evil spoken of:

17   For the kingdom of God is not meat and drink; but righteousness, and peace, and joy in the Holy Ghost.

18   For he that in these things serves Christ [is] acceptable to God, and approved of men.

19   Let us therefore follow after the things which make for peace, and things wherewith one may edify another.

20   For meat destroy not the work of God. All things indeed [are] pure; but [it is] evil for that man who eats with offence.

21   [It is] good neither to eat flesh, nor to drink wine, nor [any thing] whereby your brother stumbles, or is offended, or is made weak.

22   Have you faith? have [it] to yourself before God. Happy [is] he that condemns not himself in that thing which he allows.

23	And he that doubts is damned if he eat, because [he eats] not of faith: for whatsoever [is] not of faith is sin.

How is it that we who are in Christ Jesus so easily walk by those we know are struggling in their walk with Christ, without helping them? How is it we so easily look on others in the church and say to ourselves they gossip, or she is doing this or that? Why are we not holding our brothers and sisters in Christ up like support beams to a skyscraper? Does our God do any less for us? We the undeserving vile sinners who would still be our sin have been saved ONLY because HE first LOVED us. Why is it that we so easily act dismissively? Why is it we do not reach across the aisle and embrace those in the body of Christ as Christ embraces us? We need to be better! We need to be stronger! Our God is the God who does impossible things! If we serve such a loving God, how can we be any less loving since He took a chance on us. Some things are certainly shameful, shameful in that we dare not to listen to what Jesus is telling us about how to help someone because it might mean sacrificing something about ourselves. It might mean changing a bit of who we are.

How many times have you forgiven your sister or brother in your own family? My bet is you can not count that high. Why are you afraid to extend that circle wider? We need to be more than we are! We need to be mindful of how we act and how that is seen by others. Just as you have complained to your brother or sister about how something they did embarrassed you, we have to think about how we as brothers and sisters in CHRIST, need to be that loving, living example of Christ. Are we setting the standard of being just that? Are we an example of Jesus to others? If not we must admit we are then a stumbling block not only to our walk in Christ, but to that of others who seek to be that living example of Christ to others. Are you ready to take that next step? Are you ready to adjust your life so you can be what Christ wants for you?

Open your eyes and open your ears. What is in your life that holds you back from being that example of Christ?

Dear Lord Jesus,

I want to be a living example of You! I want others to not to see me, but the one who first loved me. I want people to see my actions and my words line up with Your Word. That they are one and the same. Lord I know you are not finished with me. Trim from me those things that need to go so that less of me and my vanity is seen so that people may see you!

In Jesus name, Amen.

DAY #44
ROMANS 15:1-7
https://www.youtube.com/watch?v=J7ep_TqVm_k

1   We then that are strong ought to bear the infirmities of the weak, and not to please ourselves.

2   Let every one of us please [his] neighbour for [his] good to edification.

3   For even Christ pleased not himself; but, as it is written, The reproaches of them that reproached you fell on me.

4   For whatsoever things were written aforetime were written for our learning, that we through patience and comfort of the scriptures might have hope.

5   Now the God of patience and consolation grant you to be likeminded one toward another according to Christ Jesus:

6   That you may with one mind [and] one mouth glorify God, even the Father of our Lord Jesus Christ.

7   Wherefore receive you one another, as Christ also received us to the glory of God.

Sometimes we forget as the body of Christ how important it is to be unified as ONE BODY. Think of this as the unifying of all of Christians. Christians are those who accept Christ Jesus as Lord and are thankful for his sacrifice for our sins. We are not perfect and we do not stop being sinners. But we do know when we sin, and we know who to confess our sins to and to beg forgiveness of.

What would happen in the world today if we lifted our mouths together to sing His praises?

Many years ago, I went to a Promise Keeper event at Syracuse University. When we arrived at the Carrier Dome they had begun to sing. As we walked towards the entrance there was an invisible wall of praise and joy that hit us. YOU FELT AS IF YOU WERE WALKING THROUGH A WALL OF GLORY! Every one of us felt that glorious wall from men singing. The attendance was estimated at over 37,000! We were simply united in our love of our savior Jesus! For Bible Study we broke down into groups of ten or less. That was thoroughly exciting and intellectually stimulating.

We should accept each other who believe and unify in our love and worship of our creator! Why? Because we are not deserving of the love that saves us. We are all unworthy—not one of us is more deserving than another of the price Christ paid for us on the cross.

Dear Lord Jesus,

Work on me Lord, that I may be one who helps in unifying the body of Christ. Lord Jesus, use me to let other Christians see how our love of You binds us together. Lord, I am nothing. You are everything. Use this to not only unify believers together, but to draw those who do not know You closer to You. May our love of you be what draws others to find You.

In Jesus name, Amen.

DAY #45
ROMANS 15:8-12

https://www.youtube.com/watch?v=9JUCPgGj-xM

8   Now I say that Jesus Christ was a minister of the circumcision for the truth of God, to confirm the promises [made] unto the fathers:

9   And that the Gentiles might glorify God for [his] mercy; as it is written, For this cause I will confess to you among the Gentiles, and sing unto your name.

10 And again he saith, Rejoice, you Gentiles, with his people.

11 And again, Praise the Lord, all you Gentiles; and laud him, all you people.

12 And again, Esaias saith, There shall be a root of Jesse, and he that shall rise to reign over the Gentiles; in him shall the Gentiles trust.

When you think about it, it is so cool that God made promises concerning us non-Jews. So where are these promises? Verse 9 refers to II Samuel 22:50 is actually a part of a song of David that appears in Psalm 18:49. "Therefore will I give thanks unto you, O LORD, among the heathen, and sing praises unto your name." This prophecy came through King David!

The prophet Isaiah wrote in chapter 11 verses 1 and 10:

And there shall come forth a rod out of the stem of Jesse, and a Branch shall grow out of his roots:... And in that day there shall be a root of Jesse, which shall stand for an ensign of the people; to it shall the Gentiles seek: and his rest shall be glorious.

God made plans so that we could know HIM! This is even in Genesis though it took Christ dying on the cross for us to grasp this.

Dear Lord Jesus!

Thank You! For YOU LOVED me long before I even admitted I needed you. Your selflessness, your love goes long beyond your sacrifice on the cross. Your word tells of a plan to save even me. Lord, Your love is so incredible! SO great! That you even thought of saving me when you found Adam hiding in his sin. Lord use me to be that light and beacon to those like me who need to know you love them.

In Jesus name, Amen.

DAY #46
ROMANS 15:13-19
https://www.youtube.com/watch?v=2FI-NVVEbMo

13   Now the God of hope fill you with all joy and peace in believing, that you may abound in hope, through the power of the Holy Ghost.

14   And I myself also am persuaded of you, my brethren, that you also are full of goodness, filled with all knowledge, able also to admonish one another.

15   Nevertheless, brethren, I have written the more boldly unto you in some sort, as putting you in mind, because of the grace that is given to me of God,

16 That I should be the minister of Jesus Christ to the Gentiles, ministering the gospel of God, that the offering up of the Gentiles might be acceptable, being sanctified by the Holy Ghost.

17 I have therefore whereof I may glory through Jesus Christ in those things which pertain to God.

18 For I will not dare to speak of any of those things which Christ hath not wrought by me, to make the Gentiles obedient, by word and deed,

19 Through mighty signs and wonders, by the power of the Spirit of God; so that from Jerusalem, and round about unto Illyricum, I have fully preached the gospel of Christ.

Only the living God can fill a person with joy! Its effects are forever lasting. Living in on hope! Living through the power of the Holy Ghost! What an incredible life changing moment that goes on and on.

Paul acknowledges these changes and the power of the Holy Ghost, Paul preaches not to the saved, but to the lost. Sharing the Good News of Jesus. Paul speaks of important things that have to exist so he can be free to evangelize rather than build up. 1) That the flock be built up in knowledge of the scriptures and knowledge of Jesus Christ. 2) That the body of Christ admonishes one another to grow and do what is right unto God. Ask yourself is your church body doing these things? Are your church members growing in the knowledge of Jesus Christ, and admonishing each other so that evangelists feel free to share God's Word?

We as members of the body of Christ, need to do our part. We need to be growing in the Lord. We need to be reading and learning the Word of God daily. We need to be admonishing each other, building each other up. We need to be helping each other grow in Christ. Ask yourself what it is that you can do to help in this manner. Are you sharing your devotions with others? Are you encouraging others to share what they learned? Are you there when your brother or sister in Christ needs you? Such simple things are essential so that the evangelists feel freed and empowered to do the work God has given them.

Dear Lord Jesus,

I so want to be that living example of You, Lord Jesus. Embolden me to share what I learn from your Word each day. Embolden me that I may be a doer of your word not just a listener to it. Use me Lord, that I may lift up my brothers and sisters in Christ when they need it most. I ask Lord, that you bless me with these things.

In Jesus name, Amen.

DAY #47
ROMANS 15:20-29

https://www.youtube.com/watch?v=Tkv_xMdaHkA

20   Yea, so have I strived to preach the gospel, not where Christ was named, lest I should build upon another man's foundation:

21   But as it is written, To whom he was not spoken of, they shall see: and they that have not heard shall understand.

22   For which cause also I have been much hindered from coming to you.

23   But now having no more place in these parts, and having a great desire these many years to come unto you;

24   Whensoever I take my journey into Spain, I will come to you: for I trust to see you in my journey, and to be brought

on my way there by you, if first I be somewhat filled with your [company].

25 But now I go unto Jerusalem to minister unto the saints.

26 For it hath pleased them of Macedonia and Achaia to make a certain contribution for the poor saints which are at Jerusalem.

27 It hath pleased them verily; and their debtors they are. For if the Gentiles have been made partakers of their spiritual things, their duty is also to minister unto them in carnal things.

28 When therefore I have performed this, and have sealed to them this fruit, I will come by you into Spain.

29 And I am sure that, when I come unto you, I shall come in the fulness of the blessing of the gospel of Christ.

Paul has the heart of an evangelist, he longs to go where no one has yet been to share God's Word and the great and glorious Gospel of our Lord Jesus Christ. He thinks about the Christians he has heard of in Rome, prays for them and longs to see them. Not to preach to the saints. He longs for their companionship, their conversation and mutual praise of our Lord.

Some commentators note how at this time many may have simply longed to see Rome in its glory. But for Paul, Rome was a stepping stone on intended journey to preach in Spain. Paul had no intention of being a tourist. A tourist looks at things. Paul longed for their company and a chance to spread the Good News to those in Spain.

Paul is following God's lead, he sees the task at hand, the field ripe for the harvest, that he might plant the seeds of the Good News for the salvation of those who do not know Jesus, that God might harvest.

Paul even speaks of those he is with presently as feeling in debt to those in Jerusalem for having sent Paul on his trip to share the news good with them. They send a financial gift to combat the prophesied great famine spoken of in Acts 11, that historical records share happened during the 4th year of Claudius Caeasar. Many died according history. The Christian tradition of generosity during times of calamity begins here. Paul shared the need of those in Jerusalem with those in places where he discipled new believers. Giving beyond tithing had to be hard considering how little most had. But whatever was given Paul returned with to bless those suffering from the lack of food.

Dear Lord Jesus,

Thank you for loving me so much, that you sent people to preach the good news so that I, even I could hear of your incredible work. Use me that I may share your glory with others through example and actions of love and kindness. Bless me Lord, that I may bless those in times of trouble. Lord God, may I be Your faithful servant, seeking to do your will.

In Jesus name, Amen.

DAY #48
ROMANS 15:30-33
https://www.youtube.com/watch?v=Y82uFB9A3V8

30   Now I beseech you, brethren, for the Lord Jesus Christ's sake, and for the love of the Spirit, that you strive together with me in [your] prayers to God for me;

31   That I may be delivered from them that do not believe in Judaea; and that my service which [I have] for Jerusalem may be accepted of the saints;

32   That I may come unto you with joy by the will of God, and may with you be refreshed.

33   Now the God of peace [be] with you all. Amen.

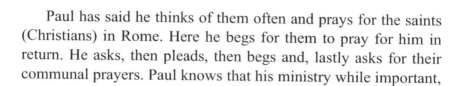

Paul has said he thinks of them often and prays for the saints (Christians) in Rome. Here he begs for them to pray for him in return. He asks, then pleads, then begs and, lastly asks for their communal prayers. Paul knows that his ministry while important, needs the prayers of others. Paul thoroughly believes that God answers prayer, and that prayer changes things.

Paul faced his accusers. He believed that God would provide and deliver him from trouble. But he knew that praying is power. This is why we need to pray for our loved ones and our leaders.

Paul continues to hope and pray that he can enjoy the company of his fellow believers in Rome. What better way tis there, for Paul to make it to Rome, and have that happen, than to have those in Rome pray for his safe travels and hopeful arrival in the future? Pray believing that God will give you what you desire. Pray hoping for what you see as God's desires, and pray knowing that God answers prayer.

Dear Lord Jesus,

Your love of me, your caring, your undeniable flood of hope, desire and love overwhelms me. You are the great planner, the incredible designer of the flowers, the clouds and so much more. Yet you take time to listen to my desires. Thank you for your love. Lord, use me that I may share this love you have. Use me that I may help others see the value in prayer.

In Jesus name, Amen.

DAY #49
ROMANS 16:1-15
https://www.youtube.com/watch?v=t22baxs7jNk

1   I commend unto you Phebe our sister, which is a servant of the church which is at Cenchrea:

2   That you receive her in the Lord, as becomes saints, and that you assist her in whatsoever business she has need of you: for she hath been a helper in time of need for many, and of myself also.

3   Greet Priscilla and Aquila my helpers in Christ Jesus:

4   Who have for my life laid down their own necks: unto whom not only I give thanks, but also all the churches of the Gentiles.

5   Likewise [greet] the church that is in their house. Salute my well beloved Epaenetus, who is the first fruits of Achaia unto Christ.

6   Greet Mary, who bestowed much labour on us.

7   Salute Andronicus and Junia, my kinsmen, and my fellow prisoners, who are of note among the apostles, who also were in Christ before me.

8   Greet Amplias my beloved in the Lord.

9   Salute Urbane, our helper in Christ, and Stachys my beloved.

10 Salute Apelles approved in Christ. Salute them which are of Aristobulus' [household].

11 Salute Herodion my kinsman. Greet them that be of the [household] of Narcissus, which are in the Lord.

12   Salute Tryphena and Tryphosa, who labour in the Lord. Salute the beloved Persis, which laboured much in the Lord.

13   Salute Rufus chosen in the Lord, and his mother and mine.

14   Salute Asyncritus, Phlegon, Hermas, Patrobas, Hermes, and the brethren which are with them.

15   Salute Philologus, and Julia, Nereus, and his sister, and Olympas, and all the saints which are with them.

Paul begins the end of his letters with introductions standard protocols of this would be in order of importance and relevance of the person(s) mentioned. Phebe is mentioned first here. This is thought because she may be the one who delivered Paul's letter to the Romans. She is unusual in that she is very independent and is seen as a woman of means and of business. Paul says more about her than anyone else in this letter. Speaking of her as a Christian first then speaks of her own personal needs, mentioning her acts of generosity that make her stand out from others. This is a woman who lives what she believes.

Priscilla and Aquilla are mentioned next. It is very unusual even back then to mention the wife before her husband. Paul is saying something to those who receive the letter here about her love of God. The husband and wife were Paul's co-workers as they were tent makers. They paid for their travels by arriving and setting up shop to go about this task. This also speaks of their being Jewish. They travelled with Paul and learned from him. Their faith in Jesus is also something they live without fear in a time when such a faith could sign your death warrant. They risked their own lives that Paul might live.

Paul says something special about each person he introduces. There is a level of kindness and a letter of introduction that communicates a deep love and respect he has for each them. As if

50 DAYS IN ROMANS

his absence from them will be an absence in his heart. Priscilla and Aquilla he will meet again, but the others?

Dear Lord Jesus,

I thank and praise you for each believer you put in my life. Lord God, let me not forget to praise you for them, nor may I forget them when we are apart. Lord give me the opportunity to recommend the believers around me to other Christians. Lord use me that I may not forget to encourage those around me to a stronger faith in you.

In Jesus name, Amen.

DAY #50
ROMANS 16:16-20
https://www.youtube.com/watch?v=av1IstgJREQ

16   Salute one another with a holy kiss. The churches of Christ salute you.

17   Now I beseech you, brethren, mark them which cause divisions and offences contrary to the doctrine which ye have learned; and avoid them.

18   For they that are such serve not our Lord Jesus Christ, but their own belly; and by good words and fair speeches deceive the hearts of the simple.

19   For your obedience is come abroad unto all [men]. I am glad therefore on your behalf: but yet I would have you wise unto that which is good, and simple concerning evil.

20   And the God of peace shall bruise Satan under your feet shortly. The grace of our Lord Jesus Christ [be] with you. Amen.

In the North East USA, it's a rare day you get greeted with a holy kiss. A hand shake works here, this is clearly something cultural, but it does make us think about how intimate we are with those we love as brothers and sisters in Christ. Here a hug feels so good. Its hard to let your brother or sister pass by you without a hug. Why? Because there is great joy in the presence of those who love you and love the Lord. It is almost empowering. Then there is one more thing. Its as if you know that hug will re-energize you to do the work you need to do. To do whatever task that may be coming.

Even in the first years after Jesus died on the cross there were some who sought to distort to break the church with lies, division, and false doctrine. Some sought to please only themselves or were led by the devil alone. Yet, knowing those things it was absolutely essential to keep them out of the church and to avoid them. Even today these truths ring true. It is why there is great importance in a church's doctrinal statement.

The last sentence of this letter of Paul speaks of the fulfillment of Genesis 3:15. God's prophecy given to Adam and Eve fulfilled in the person Jesus Christ, the Messiah, the incredible wonder working loving God.

Dear Lord Jesus,

May I never forget the incredible blessings poured out on me through my brothers and sisters in Christ. May I never forget how they are my family! They are a part of what makes me, me. Lord watch over them for their presence, comfort, and words enable to me stand for You! Lord, their love of me is an expression of your love for them! It is something I feel down into my bones. Lord use me, your servant, that I may be one who shines a light so others may see your love for them even while they are sinners.

In Jesus name, Amen.

I hope you enjoyed this devotional and the linked videos as much as I enjoyed putting this study together to share with you.

If you are looking for a someone to share God's Word with you and your flock I can be reached at http://paulsutliff.com.

Made in the USA
Monee, IL
22 September 2024